A RUSSIAN SONG BOOK

Edited by Rose N. Rubin and Michael Stillman

Introduction by Henrietta Yurchenco

Published in Association with Miro Music Inc., New York, by
DOVER PUBLICATIONS, INC., NEW YORK

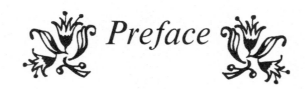

Preface

THE GENERAL INTEREST in international folk music has increased tremendously during the past decade. Magazines are devoted to research on folk music; musicologists are busy with monographs; and the modern long-playing record has brought folk music of the world into the living room. Though a great deal has been written about Russian folk music the lack of available sheet music in any popular form has inevitably kept most of it out of reach of the many who would like to perform it themselves. Similarly, Russian popular songs have been unavailable, and most of them are presented here for the first time in any American collection.

The songs in this volume represent the editors' choice primarily on the basis of popularity. The selections were made from hundreds of songs and, in all instances, Soviet editions were used to obtain versions as authentic as possible. The folk songs have been arranged in easy-to-play settings utilizing keys for comfortable singing. The popular songs are somewhat more difficult in that they are "composed" songs, and it is frequently advisable to follow the composer's intentions as much as possible. The additions of the guitar chords, the use of simple harmonic structure and the general instrumental treatment are intended to assist the song-lover.

It is suggested that listening to the recordings of these songs will help to establish the style of rendition, the correct tempos and, of course, the correct Russian pronunciation for those who need it.

R. N. R.
M. S.

English Translations by Jerry Silverman
(with the assistance of Helen and Bill Silverman)
Piano Arrangements and Guitar Chords by Jerry Silverman
Decorations by Warren Chappell

This Dover edition, first published in 1989, is an unabridged republication of the work originally published by Random House, N.Y., 1962, in an oblong format. The present edition, in a new format, with corrections and with a specially updated discography, is published in association with Miro Music Inc., 10 Fiske Place, Mount Vernon, N.Y. 10550.

DOVER MUSICAL ARCHIVES

Library of Congress Cataloging-in-Publication Data

A Russian song book.

    Includes words in Russian and Russian romanized.
    Reprint, with updated discography. Originally published: New York : Random House, c1962.
    Discography: p.
    1. Folk music—Soviet Union. 2. Folk-songs, Russian—Soviet Union.
3. Popular music—Soviet Union. I. Rubin, Rose N. II. Stillman, Michael. III. Silverman, Jerry.
M1756.R883 1989   89-751569
ISBN-13: 978-0-486-26118-8
ISBN-10: 0-486-26118-2

Manufactured in the United States by LSC Communications
4500050301
www.doverpublications.com

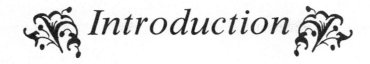 # Introduction

 SINCE THE NINETEENTH CENTURY the Western world has become acquainted with the richness of Russian folk song mainly through the symphonic and operatic works and songs of her leading composers, who have woven these splendid tunes into the fabric of their own creations. The melodies which express emotional extremes, from limitless joy to heart-rending grief, have always struck a responsive chord in people everywhere. Those who have taken the trouble to locate the text have found poetry of equal beauty laced with bold and dramatic imagery.

Where do these songs come from and under what circumstances were they born? The answers to these questions lie in the colorful background of Russia's ancient pagan mythology, her bizarre epic figures, her turbulent history and the varied folk ways of both city and country.

FESTIVALS

If we were to judge Russia by her festivals, we might say that she was a most pious Christian nation. The festivals of Easter, Christmas, Shrovetide, St. John's, Annunciation and Trinity were important and widespread, but many of the songs, dances and rituals originated in pagan times when pantheistic gods held sway over the Slavic tribes.

For the peasant, Christmas was the favorite season. The hard work of the harvest was over, the larder full to the brim, and the barn stocked with fat geese, cows and pigs. Peasants masqueraded as goats, bulls, bears and wolves, entertaining everyone with their antics. The Kolyadki, special songs for Christmas and New Year's, and dancing were performed at all village festivities. The spring holidays, in which the death of winter is acted out and the earth's rebirth heralded, were eagerly awaited by everyone.

From the first of March the peasants would dance and sing to hurry the spring along. Women and children would go to the hills or climb to the roofs of their barns and there sing the season's evocations:

Spring, beautiful Spring!
Come, O Spring, with joy
With great goodness:
With deep roots,
With abundant corn!

On March ninth, the larks were supposed to arrive. Groups of girls sang at opposite ends of the village, one chorus joyously answering the other in the dance-choral song known as *khorovod.*

O you larks,
Dear little larks,
Fly into the field,
Bring health:
First for the cows,
Second, the sheep,
Third for man.

Other days were celebrated, like the arrival of the cuckoo and the swallow, the emergence of the bear from his winter lair, the day the river ice began to break up, so that "The Pike can send its tail through it."

The merrymaking of spring reached its climax in Trinity Day. About this time the peasants stopped work to greet the return of the *Rusalkas,* or female water spirits, who have long been a subject of great fascination for writers and composers. The peasants feared and loved the *Rusalkas,* for they embodied both good and evil. To placate these restless ancestral spirits they offered them songs, dances, lovely garlands of flowers and many ceremonials. When the people tired of them, a *khorovod* was performed, a straw figure representing the *Rusalkas* was burned and they disappeared until the next spring.

Midsummer's Night, honoring St. John the Baptist (Kupalo the Bather), ended the spring cycle of ceremonies. The rituals, games and songs were a combination of merrymaking and lamentation, while bonfires roared, wild dancing and joyful songs (*kupalskiya*) were performed all through the night. A sixteenth-century observer was shocked by the proceedings: "They sang Satanic songs," he wrote, "and danced, and the Devil danced for joy with them, and they prayed to him and magnified him, and forgot God." Now, Midsummer Night, celebrated not only in Russia but all over Europe, is a rather tame affair but is universally loved by city and country folk. Such works as *Night on Bald Mountain* by Mussorgsky and Stravinsky's *Petrouchka* were inspired by the tunes and customs of the occasion.

When spring holidays ended, the Russians returned to the fields until harvest festivities. Then they sang of the hard labor of reaping, praise to the landowners, and the serf's toil for his lord. One of the beautiful harvest songs honored the spirit of the field, a he-goat, who was believed to hide in the last sheaf of grain:

> The he-goat lies by the boundary line
> And admires his beard;
> And whose is this beard,
> All dripping with honey,
> And all garlanded with silk?

Harvest ends the year's cycle of agricultural festivals.

FUNERAL CHANTS—ZAPLACHKI

Funeral ceremonies and chants go back to tribal times. Their function was to prevent the dead person's return and to placate him with offerings, thereby assuring his comfortable passage to another world. Professional wailers were important figures and respected throughout Russia for their musical and poetic gifts. The most famous wailer of the 1890's, Irina Fedosova, completely involved in her performance, entered personally into the mourners' grief. On one occasion she sang in the name of the widow at the funeral of a drunkard. Unable to find words of praise for the dead man, she spoke the honest truth:

> I have gone through the licensed taverns,
> I have stood around by the public houses;
> Looking at his spendings, I have trembled,
> I have called upon him who should be my hope,
>   I have humiliated myself.
> I, miserable one, have heard enough of humiliation,
> I have endured heavy beating;
> He shamed me, he dishonored me before good people.

WEDDING SONGS

Of all the songs which have come down to us from ancient times, none are more beautiful than those connected with weddings. Each ceremony, from the marriage broker's first visit to the bride's home to the wedding itself, is described in chants of matchless poetry and melody. As in a well-constructed play, the chief characters—bride, bridegroom, best man, wedding guests, and the professional wailer—enact their various roles.

When the matchmaker has concluded his arrangements, it is the custom for the girl to beg her parents to break off the engagement. Her sentiments are contained in this song:

> Not two ravens have flown together in the dark forest,
> Nor have two warriors ridden together in the open
>   plain,
> But two matchmakers have met within my home . . .

When this playacting, always performed with great sincerity, is over, presents are exchanged between the families and a gay feast is held. The songs for this occasion are lyrical and romantic:

> The nightingale flew
> To the coppice green,
> To the birchwoods bright.
> To a spray, without heeding,
> The nightingale flew.

It was traditional for the bride to bewail the loss of girlhood freedom and decry the prospect of living with a strange family, even if it was a love match. This chant is typical warning by the bride's sister:

> Don't expect my dear sister
> That your father-in-law will wake you up gently,
> That your mother-in-law will give orders nicely.
> They will howl at you like wild beasts
> And they will hiss at you like snakes.

Before the wedding the two families exchange visits characterized by eating, dancing and singing. On these social occasions the wailer would sing in praise of the guests. Here is the conclusion of one, a paean to the bridegroom:

> He sits there bright as a burning taper;
> When he speaks it is like the giving of rubles.
> His ruddiness is taken from the sun,
> His fairness from the white snow.
> His cheeks are like the crimson poppy,
> His bright eyes are the eyes of a hawk,
> His brows are black with the blackness of sable.

While many customs are no longer observed, the chief wedding guest still serves as jester and merrymaker. Here is a modern song, a perfect combination of new and old, in which he enumerates the groom's worldly goods:

> He has a great many servants,
> He has bright falcons,
> Swift eagles,
> Hunting dogs,
> Mounted Cossacks,
> Leaping animals,
> And birds that peck.
> He has motorboats
> And others that are submarines.
> Of course there are airplanes . . .

BYLINY AND HISTORICAL SONGS

In the middle ages so-called buffoons and clowns used to appear in city squares and village streets to sing byliny, the long poems of Russia's heroes and great national events. They were no ordinary street entertainers despite their unruly behavior and lack of reverence for authority. They were popular poets and musicians with extraordinary gifts. So disarming was their art that boyars (aristocrats), princes and even tzars forgot their disapproval and admitted them to their palaces to provide entertainment.

The northern peasantry developed a particular predilection for this stately storyteller's art. *Byliny* were passed on from father to son, and the best of them knew thousands of verses by heart. Even when they performed before vast audiences they were impassioned and wholly involved in the events they related.

Back in the 1890's a schoolteacher once asked the famous reciter I. T. Ryabinin to delete certain "indecent" verses from an epic poem he was about to deliver. The singer answered: "But how can I help singing it? Would you take away a word of the song? Because it is an ancient one, and as the men of old used to sing it, so we must sing it. You know yourself, it was not composed by us, and it will not end with us." What a direct statement of the meaning and dignity of tradition!

The ancient *byliny,* first written down in the seventeenth century, go back at least a thousand years. The drama of medieval Russia unfolds in epic poems about such historical figures as Vaska Buslayev, a reckless but bold fighter; the sorceress Marinka, personification of evil; the Russian Robin Hood, Ilya of Murom; and Sadko, the subject of Rimsky-Korsakov's opera, the lowly zither player endowed with miraculous powers.

By the middle of the sixteenth century, the creation of *byliny* had about ended and the new, shorter, less ceremonial historical ballads came into existence. These told of the reign of Ivan the Terrible, and the peasant revolt a half century later led by Stepan Razin. A unique place in Russian folklore is held by Razin, if only for the sheer weight of songs written about him.

Like the earlier heroes, Ivan and Razin were larger-than-life-size men, exercising extraordinary powers like the warding off of bullets and charming poisonous snakes. The ballads always justify even their outrageous acts. In one song describing the capture of Astrakhan it says:

> *Stenka Razin rushed to the corner tower,*
> *And with a great roll he threw the governor down,*
> *And all his little children he hung up by the feet.*

Two Razin ballads are included in this book: *"Stenka Razin"* (From Beyond the Island), in which he tosses the Queen of Persia into the Volga to reassure his men that he has not deserted them for a woman, and "The Cliff on the Volga," which lauds his fearlessness.

Later on, many Razin stories were reworked for an eighteenth-century rebel leader, Yemelyan Pugachev, who fought against serfdom, and for Peter the Great, who was also admired by the Russian populace. The entrance of Russia into European affairs brought more changes in her folklore. The hardships of the long twenty-five-year military conscription service imposed by Peter the Great gave rise to military recruit songs and lamentations. The heart-rending songs of the disruption of family life and work are among Russia's finest creations.

Also typical were the robust, rhythmical campaign and marching tunes which praised military valor and described the exploits of famous Russian generals. Among the best known are those about General Suvorov, who fought in the Russo-Turkish Wars and, incidentally, put down the Pugachev peasant rebellion of 1775! Although these songs can be considered a continuation of the old historical narrative ballads, in poetic and musical design they anticipated the nineteenth century. Many of them, as well as ancient ritual peasant songs, became popular in the cities, and even in the court, where Italian and French music were currently enjoying great vogue. Such musicians as the gusli* player Vassily Trutovsky, one of Russia's first folk-song collectors, and the composer Khandoshkin served in the court of Catherine II in the dual capacity of folk singers and artists in the classical tradition.

LYRIC SONGS

Lyric songs, in contrast to narrative and ritual songs, are essentially emotional expressions of feeling. Old and young sang them at home, in the fields, as solo and in chorus. They were created by people of all walks of life—the peasantry, barge haulers, stagecoach drivers, soldiers, robbers (many of whom were peasant fugitives from serfdom), city artisans and merchants. During the autumn and winter the village girls would gather together of an evening. At these *posidyelki* they would do their spinning, singing and gossiping as they worked. A woman's heavy lot, domination by a husband, or the misfortunes of an arranged marriage, love and jealousy were favorite themes.

Ladies of the upper classes also had their songs. The melodies borrowed heavily from peasant music but the words were steeped in the perfumed and sentimental atmosphere of the Parisian boudoir.

The lyric songs are by far the most popular and numerous in both new and old Russia. "Kalinka" (Little Snowball Bush), "Troika Rushing," "Snow Flurries," "Monotonously Rings the Little Coach Bell," and "In the Meadow Stood a Little Birch Tree," included in this volume, are among the best known, and deservedly so, for they are perfect melodic and poetic gems. The lyrics are combinations of stock formulas, symbolism and imagery culled from ancient sources—the *byliny,* the laments of the wailers, proverbs and riddles. They represent Russian folk song in its most personal and intimate aspect.

NINETEENTH-CENTURY INDUSTRIAL FOLKLORE

While lyric songs were familiar to all, new satirical and often bitter songs became popular with the then small but expanding class of industrial workers. These described the dreadful conditions of child labor and the prison-like regimes of the mines. "Bandit" songs were composed by escaped criminals and workers who fled to live in the hills.

Many songs of the time reflected peasant expectations of patriarchal benevolence from their new employers. Thus,

---

* A Russian stringed instrument of the dulcimer type.

in one song, when the workers complain, the mill owner answers:

> Do not weep now, fine young fellows, fine young
> factory workers,
> I will build for you, my children, two bright new
> looms,
> Authentic looms, heavy threads for the warp,
> And I will give to you, children, a fine high price
> A fine high price, napkins at a ruble a piece.

The peasant first idealized city existence. By contrast with the uneventful life of the village, the city, with its taverns, beautiful girls, tailored clothes and fine carriages, must have seemed like heaven itself. In one delightful song a country boy writes a letter to the "kingdom of Moscow":

> The village of Voronkovskaya
> Is an accursed settlement.
> I may call it a prison.

Later on, his imagination takes him to the coveted city:

> Now I live in Moscow,
> In Moscow I live, and have my abode;
> I am not indifferent to the beautiful girls,
> And I go to the tavern with them.

With greater mechanization in the factories, the romance of city life began to pall. Plans for revolt inspired new songs. Now the worker looked back on peasant life as the superior way of living. Thus:

> In the summer, at his work in the field
> He is his own master.
> In the winter he sleeps like a log without waking,
> Like a great lord.

By the end of the nineteenth century the songs were battle cries to revolution. More and more they were based on popular tunes and ballads rather than on peasant melodies. Many revolutionary songs composed by musicians and writers became part of the workers own repertory. One of the finest of these, "Dubinushka," is included here.

AFTER THE REVOLUTION

The songs heard during the period between the two wars were serious and purposeful. Those of pre-revolutionary years, known principally to city workers, now were disseminated throughout the entire nation. Soldiers returning from the front, students, peasant leaders and officials brought them to every village and hamlet. More songs came from the pens of well-known composers and poets, but the unlettered people continued to create their own, based on old melodies. Partisan poets showed an excellent knowledge of traditional peasant material in their revisions of old songs. For "On the Death of Pogadayev," they used the opening of the ballad "The Sea Gulls," which starts with these beautiful lines:

> Now the morning has dawned red, the waters are
> growing rosy,
> Above the lake flies a swift sea gull.

Transformed by the partisans it began:

> Now the morning has dawned red, we have occupied
> Sretensk
> And with fighting the enemy has withdrawn from
> the town
> But we have lost the commander of the regiment.
> The corpse of the slain man—we could not find it.
> All night long we wandered there in battle, among
> the mounds
> In the ravines, standing waist-deep in the cold
> snow. . .

Many songs were written of the changes taking place on the home front—the NEP period (New Economic Policy), the independence of women, etc. Here is one in praise of farm collectivization:

> The little samovars reached the boiling point,
> The little teapots started to clatter,
> All the collective farmers began to sing,
> The kulaks burst into tears.

With increased literacy came a blending of traditional oral poetry and literature.

POPULAR MUSIC IN THE POSTWAR PERIOD

Immediately after the war, more patriotic songs about its heroes and battles appeared. Although bitter memories were still fresh in the people's minds, the task of rebuilding occupied everyone's energies. Soviet songwriters began to write new tunes and words about peacetime pursuits in factories and collective farms.

Still on the serious side were student songs and marches performed at the various international youth congresses. Even Khatchaturian wrote music for these occasions. The tunes for the first three postwar congresses were calls to battle, but those written for the later meetings were softer. Now the young people danced polkas, mazurkas and waltzes, and sang lyric songs and barcarolles.

Until the last few years Soviet popular music was cut off from important trends in Europe and the United States. Today, dance halls, theaters, clubs and movies are ringing with jazzy and continental tunes like "Moscow Nights," by V. Soloviev-Sedoy; "Lonely Accordion," by B. Mokroussov; and "Katiusha," by M. Blanter, which are included in this book.

The finest composers also devote themselves to the writing of popular songs. Shostakovich's "Song of Greeting," Knipper's "Meadowlands" (originally the final movement of his Fourth Symphony) and Zakharov's "Who Knows Why?" are some of the best examples. In factories and village collectives amateur songwriters add to the repertory of Russian songs—even as did their forebears through the ages.

MUSICAL CHARACTERISTICS

Russia's folk music follows the pattern of her history. In rhythm, melody and polyphonic treatment can be seen the basic Slavic element and the contribution from Byzantine and Mongolian cultures. Although other Slavic nations show decided influence from Northern and Western Europe, Russia, until the nineteenth century, shows surprisingly little.

Melodies and dance steps owe their rhythms not to the regular division of beats into measures but to the flow of poetic meter. Thus such alternations as 3/4 with 2/4, 4/4 with 5/4, and 7/4 with 2/4 are common in many songs.

It has been said too often and by experts who should know better that Russian folk music is characteristically in minor key. This is not true. The melodies, simple in structure, are roughly divided into major, minor, alternations of major and minor, medieval church modes, ancient pentatonic, and uncertain modality (combinations of many modes).

Tchaikovsky's remarks on the nature of Russian folk songs are worth quoting here. In a letter to Tolstoy acknowledging the receipt of some songs, he wrote: "I must frankly say the songs have not been skillfully treated, and thereby all their original beauty has been lost. The chief fault is, there they have been forced into a regular formal rhythm. Besides this, the greater part of these songs is written in the cheerful D-major scale, and this does not agree in the least with the tonality of the true Russian Volkslied, which is always of an uncertain tonality, so that one can really only compare with the old church modes."

The *khorovod,* or basic dance-choral song, sung *a cappella,* for all festive occasions, is the Russian form of folk polyphony. No doubt it has its roots in primitive Byzantine church music and the thirteenth-century Znamenny chant, which apparently was written in two parts. First one voice sings the melody, then other voices in succession join in to sing variants of the same melody in a free association, thereby creating a kind of counterpoint.

HENRIETTA YURCHENCO

Guide to Transliteration

There is no universally accepted system of transliterating the Cyrillic alphabet.

The system used in this book is that used by the Library of Congress.

Cyrillic alphabet	Transliteration	As In
а	a	far
б	b	back
в	v	visa
г	g	good
д	d	done
е	e	yet
ж	zh	measure
з	z	zoo
и	i	knee
й	ĭ	boy
к	k	kit
л	l	bell
м	m	ham
н	n	nose
о	o	port

Cyrillic alphabet	Transliteration	As In
п	p	part
р	r	rose
с	s	steal
т	t	tar
у	u	toot
ф	f	fall
х	kh	howl (strongly aspirated)
ц	ts	mats
ч	ch	chin
ш	sh	shun
щ	shch	mesh chain
ъ	″	(hard sign — no sound)
ы	y	syllable
ь	′	(soft sign — no sound)
э	e	every
ю	iu	youth
я	ia	yard
ё	yo	yon

Contents

DOWN ALONG
THE MOTHER VOLGA

ВНИЗ ПО МАТУШКЕ ПО ВОЛГЕ

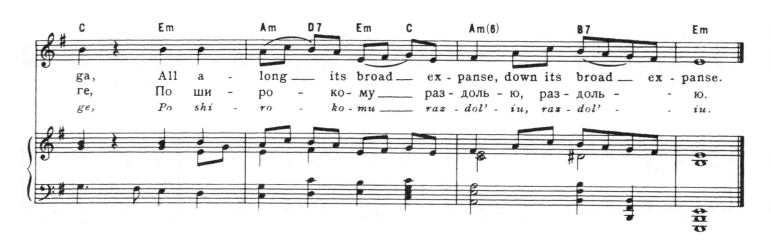

2. All along its broad expanse—
   expanse
   Heavy weather was a-rising—
   a-rising.

3. Heavy weather was a-ris—a-rising,
   Not a little storm was brewing—
   was brewing.

2. По широкому раздо...
   раздолью,
   Поднималась непого...
   непогода.

3. Поднималась непого...
   непогода,
   Погодушка немала...немалая.

2. *Po shirokomu razdo... razdol'iu,*
   Podnimalas' nepogo... nepogoda.

3. *Podnimalas' nepogo... nepogoda,*
   Pogodushka nemala... nemalaia.

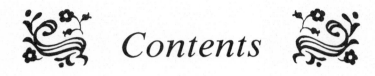

Contents

 # Part I: Folk Songs

DOWN THE VOLGA RIVER

ВНИЗ ПО ВОЛГЕ-РЕКЕ

Broadly

Down the Vol — ga's broad stream   From Nizh —
Вниз по Вол — ге ре — ке,   С Нижня—
Vniz po Vol — ge re — ke,   S Nizh — nia—

ni — Nov-go — rod   A stout riv — er—
Нов—го—ро—да   Сна—ря—жён стру—
Nov — go—ro — da   Sna—ria—zhën stru—

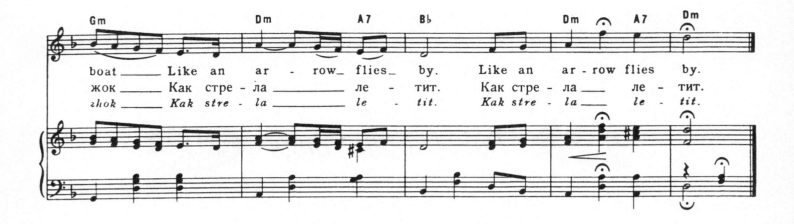

boat _____ Like an ar - row _ flies _ by. Like an ar - row flies by.
жок _____ Как стре - ла _____ ле - тит. Как стре - ла _ ле - тит.
zhok _____ Kak stre - la _____ le - tit. Kak stre - la _ le - tit.

2. Well, now, on that stout boat,
   That was loaded down,
   Forty-two dauntless oarsmen
   Sat and rowed with all their might.

3. Well, now, one of the men,
   A brave young lad,
   In deep thought was lost,
   Downcast was his eye.

4. "Say, oh, why do you sit,
   My stout-hearted lad,
   Lost in deep reverie,
   And with downcast eye?"

5. "My thoughts you shall know,
   Why I do grieve so.
   All about one soul,
   A beautiful maid.

6. "Oh, my brothers, all,
   My comrades in toil,
   Do for me, I pray,
   This devoted deed.

7. "Throw me overboard
   To Mother Volga.
   Drown then deep in her
   All my pain and woe."

2. Как на том на стружке,
   На снаряженном,
   Удалых гребцов
   Сорок два сидят.

3. Как один из них,
   Добрый молодец,
   Призадумался,
   Пригорюнился.

4. «Ах, о чём же ты,
   Добрый молодец,
   Призадумался,
   Пригорюнился?»

5. «Я задумался,
   Пригорюнился,
   Об одной душе,
   Красной девице.

6. «Эх вы, братцы мои,
   Вы, товарищи,
   Сослужите вы мне
   Службу верную.

7. «Киньте, бросьте меня
   В Волгу-матушку,
   Утопите в ней
   Грусть тоску мою.»

2. *Kak na tom na struzhke,
   Na snariazhennom,
   Udalykh grebtsov
   Sorok dva sidiat.*

3. *Kak odin iz nikh,
   Dobryi molodets,
   Prizadumalsia,
   Prigoriunilsia.*

4. *"Akh, o chëm zhe ty,
   Dobryi molodets,
   Prizadumalsia,
   Prigoriunilsia?"*

5. *"Ia zadumalsia,
   Prigoriunilsia,
   Ob odnoi dushe,
   Krasnoi devitse.*

6. *"Ekh vy, bratsy moi,
   Vy, tovarishchi,
   Sosluzhite vy mne
   Sluzhbu vernuiu.*

7. *"Kin'te, bros'te menia
   V Volgu-matushku,
   Utopite v nei
   Grust' tosku moiu."*

OH, YOU DEAR LITTLE NIGHT

АХ ТЫ, НОЧЕНЬКА

Oh, you dear lit-tle night._____ Oh, you__
Ах ты, но - чень - ка._____ Ноч - ка__
Akh ty, no - chen' - ka._____ Noch - ka__

dark__ lit-tle night._____ Oh, you au - tumn__
тём - на - я._____ Ноч - ка тём - на
tëm - na - ia._____ Noch - ka tëm - na -

night._____ Oh, you dark__ au - tumn night._____ night._____
я,_____ ночь о - сен - ня - я _____ я
ia._____ Noch' o - sen - nia - ia._____ ia.

2. With whom on this night,
   With whom this dark night,
   With whom this autumn night,
   Oh, shall I pass the time?

3. I have no father,
   I have no mother,
   And I only have
   One to call my own.

4. But we do not live
   Peacefully as one,
   Peacefully as one,
   And there is no joy.

2. С кем я ноченьку, с кем я тёмную,
   С кем осеннюю коротать буду.

3. Нет ни батюшки, нет ни матушки,
   Только есть у меня мил сердечный друг.

4. Да и тот со мной не в ладу живёт,
   Не в ладу живёт, не в согласии.

2. *S kem ia nochen'ku, s kem ia tëmnuiu,
   S kem osenniuiu korotat' budu.*

3. *Net ni batiushki, net ni matushki,
   Tol'ko est' u menia mil serdechnyi drug.*

4. *Da i tot so mnoi ne v ladu zhivët,
   Ne v ladu zhivët, ne v soglasii.*

DOWN ALONG
THE MOTHER VOLGA

ВНИЗ ПО МАТУШКЕ ПО ВОЛГЕ

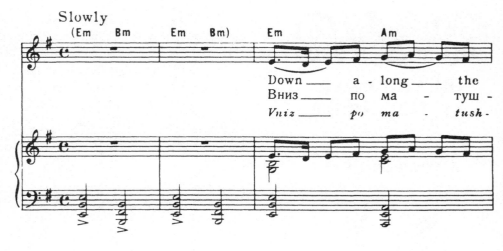

Slowly

Down a-long__ the Moth-er Vol—,__ the Vol - - - - ga, All a-long__ its broad__ ex-panse, down its broad__ ex-panse.

Вниз__ по ма-туш-ке__ по Вол—, по Вол - - - - ге, По ши-ро-ко-му__ раз-доль-ю, раз-доль - - ю.

Vniz__ po ma-tush-ke__ po Vol—, po Vol - - - - ge, Po shi-ro-ko-mu__ raz-dol'-iu, raz-dol' - - iu.

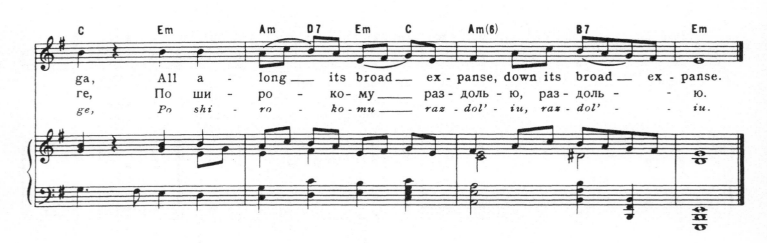

2. All along its broad expanse—
      expanse
   Heavy weather was a-rising—
      a-rising.

3. Heavy weather was a-ris—a-rising,
   Not a little storm was brewing—
      was brewing.

2. По широкому раздо . . .
      раздолью,
   Поднималась непого . . .
      непогода.

3. Поднималась непого . . .
      непогода,
   Погодушка немала . . . немалая.

2. *Po shirokomu razdo . . . razdol'iu,*
   Podnimalas' nepogo . . . nepogoda.

3. *Podnimalas' nepogo . . . nepogoda,*
   Pogodushka nemala . . . nemalaia.

4. Not a little storm was brew—
   was brewing,
   Swirling, bringing frothy waves—
   bringing frothy waves.

5. O'er the waves one can see nothing
   —see nothing,
   Nothing but a little sailboat—
   a sailboat.

6. Nothing but a little sail—
   a sailboat.
   With one white sail faintly seen—
   faintly seen.

7. (*Repeat first verse*)

4. Погодушка немала . . . немалая,
   Немалая, волнова . . . волновая.

5. Ничего в волнах не видно, не
   видно,
   Одна лодочка чернеет, чернеет.

6. Одна лодочка чернеет, чернеет,
   Только паруса белеют,
   белеют . . .

7. (Повторить первый куплет)

4. *Pogodushka nemala . . . nemalaia,*
   Nemalaia, volnova . . . volnovaia.

5. *Nichevo v volnakh ne vidno, ne*
   vidno,
   Odna lodochka cherneet, cherneet.

6. *Odna lodochka cherneet, cherneet,*
   Tol'ko parusa beleiut, beleiut . . .

7. (*Repeat first verse*)

DUBINUSHKA

ДУБИНУШКА

Moderately

Man-y songs have I heard in my own na-tive
Мно-го пе-сен слы-хал я в род-ной сто-ро-
Mno-go pe-sen sly-khal ia v rod-noi sto-ro-

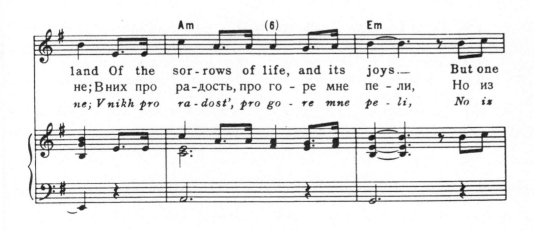

land Of the sor-rows of life, and its joys.— But one
не; В них про ра-дость, про го-ре мне пе-ли, Но из
ne; V nikh pro ra-dost', pro go-re mne pe-li, No iz

song in my mem-'ry for - ev - er will stand, That's the song of the work gang, my boys. ___
пе - сен од-на в па-мять вре - за-лась мне, Э - то пе-сня ра-бо-чей ар - те - ли. ___
pe - sen od-na v pa-miat' vre - za-las' mne, E - to pe-snia ra-bo-chei ar - te - li. ___

CHORUS
Twice as fast

Hey,   you   sledge - ham - mer,   way   oh!   Hey,   just   see   how   by   her -
Эх,   ду - би - нуш - ка,   ух - нем!   Эх,   зе - лё - на - я   са -
Ekh,   du - bi - nush - ka,   ukh - nem!   Ekh,   ze - lë - na - ia   sa -

self   she   goes. Strike   hard - er, strike   hard - er!   A - way   oh!
ма   пой - дёт!   По - дёр - нем,   по - дёр - нем,   да   ух - нем!
ma   poi - dët!   Po - dër - nem,   po - dër - nem,   Da   ukh - nem!

2. And from grandpa to father, from
   father to son,
   Like a precious bequest our song
   goes.
   And whenever the work becomes
   too hard for one,
   Our hammer we thank for its strong
   blows.
   (Chorus)

2. И от дедов к отцам, от отцов
   к сыновьям
   Эта песня идёт по наследству.
   И как только работать нам
   станет невмочь,
   Мы — к дубине, как к верному
   средству.

2. I ot dedov k otsam, ot otsov k
   synov'iam
   Eta pesnia idët po nasledstvu.
   I kak tol'ko rabotat' nam stanet
   nevmoch',
   My — k dubine, kak k vernomu
   sredstvu.

3. When I first heard this song it was sung by a gang
   As they hoisted a huge beam together.
   All at once the beam slipped—down it crashed with a bang;
   Two boys crushed, their song silenced forever.
   (*Chorus*)

4. Whether towing a bargeload of iron or wood,
   With toiling behind and before us.
   Or when suffering with pain in our breast, it is good
   To sing of our hammer in chorus.
   (*Chorus*)

5. And when by the Volga we sink in the sand,
   And along its steep banks we do clamber,
   And our very breath stops and we can't even stand,
   Then we sing once again of our hammer.
   (*Chorus*)

6. But the time it will come, oh, my brothers, it's near,
   When we'll rise with an earth-shaking clamor.
   For the lords and the Czar and the priests, never fear,
   We will find us a much stronger hammer.
   (*Chorus*)

3. Я слыхал эту песнь, её пела артель,
   Поднимая бревно на стропила.
   Вдруг бревно сорвалось, и умолкла артель,
   Двух здоровых парней придавило.
   (*Chorus*)

4. Тянем с лесом судно иль железо куём,
   Иль в Сибири руду добываем,
   С му́кой, с болью в груди одну песню поём,
   Про дубину мы с ней вспоминаем.
   (*Chorus*)

5. И на Волге-реке, утопая в песке,
   Мы ломаем и ноги, и спину,
   Надрываем там грудь и, чтоб легче тянуть,
   Мы поём про родную дубину.
   (*Chorus*)

6. Но настанет пора, и проснётся народ,
   Разогнёт он могучую спину,
   И на бар и царя, на попов и господ
   Он отыщет покрепче дубину.
   (*Chorus*)

3. *Ia slykhal etu pesn', eë pela artel',*
   Podnimaia brevno na stropila.
   Vdrug brevno sorvalos', i umolkla artel',
   Dvukh zdorovykh parnei pridavilo.
   (*Chorus*)

4. *Tianem s lesom sudno il' zhelezo kuëm,*
   Il' v Sibiri rudu dobyvaem,
   S mukoi, s bol'iu v grudi odnu pesniu poëm,
   Pro dubinu my s nei vspominaem.
   (*Chorus*)

5. *I na Volge-reke, utopaia v peske,*
   My lomaem i nogi, i spinu,
   Nadryvaem tam grud' i, chtob legche tianut',
   My poëm pro rodnuiu dubinu.
   (*Chorus*)

6. *No nastanet pora, i prosnëtsia narod,*
   Razognët on moguchuiu spinu,
   I na bar i tsaria, na popov i gospod
   On otyshchet pokrepche dubinu.
   (*Chorus*)

THE SLENDER MOUNTAIN ASH

ТОНКАЯ РЯБИНА

words by I. SURIKOV

Moderate waltz-time

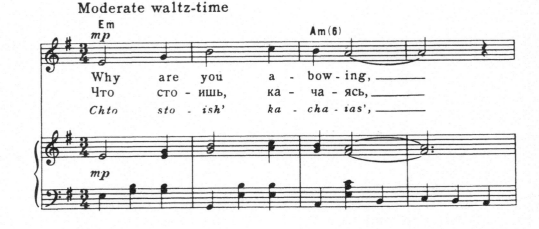

Why are you a-bow-ing, ___
Что сто - ишь, ка - ча - ясь, ___
Chto sto - ish' ka - cha - ias',

Slen - der moun - tain ro - wan, ___
Тон - ка - я ря - би - на, ___
Ton - ka - ia ria - bi - na,

Bend - ing your head down ___ To the ver - y ground? ___
Го - ло - вой скло - ня - ясь ___ До са - мо - го ты - на? ___
Go - lo - voi sklo - nia - ias' ___ *Do sa - mo - vo ty - na?* ___

2. And across the highway,
Over the wide river,
Standing just as lonely,
A tall oak hope does give her.

3. How can I, a rowan,
Get to that great oak tree,
Then I would not have to
Bow and sway so lonely.

2. А через дорогу,
За рекой широкой
Так же одиноко
Дуб стоит высокий.

3. Как бы мне, рябине,
К дубу перебраться,
Я б тогда не стала
Гнуться и качаться.

2. *A cherez dorogu,*
Za rekoi shirokoi
Tak zhe odinoko
Dub stoit vysokii.

3. *Kak by mne, riabine,*
K dubu perebrat'sia,
Ia b togda ne stala
Gnut'sia i kachat'sia.

4. With my slender branches
   I would press him tightly.
   And with our leaves twining,
   Whisper daily—nightly.

4. Тонкими ветвями
   Я б к нему прижалась
   И с его листами
   День и ночь шепталась.

4. *Tonkimi vetviami*
   Ia b k nemu prizhalas'
   I s evo listami
   Den' i noch' sheptalas'.

5. But the little rowan
   Cannot cross the river.
   Seems its fate is settled:
   Sway alone forever.

5. Но нельзя рябине
   К дубу перебраться . . .
   Знать, судьба такая —
   Век одной качаться.

5. *No nel'zia riabine*
   K dubu perebrat'sia . . .
   Znat', sud'ba takaia—
   Vek odnoi kachat'sia.

6. (*Repeat first verse*)

6. (Повторить первый куплет)

6. (*Repeat first verse*)

FAREWELL TO HAPPINESS

ПРОЩАЙ, РАДОСТЬ

Fare-well, hap - pi-ness, light of my life,
Про-щай ра - дость, жи - знь мо-я,
Pro-shchai ra - dost', zhiz-n' mo-ia,

I hear you are leav-ing me.
Слы-шу е-дешь без ме-ня.
Sly-shu e-desh' bez men-ia.

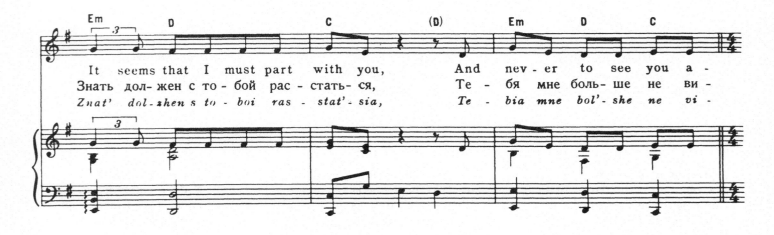

It seems that I must part with you,   And nev-er to see you a-
Знать дол-жен с то-бой рас-стать-ся,   Те-бя мне боль-ше не ви-
Znat' dol-zhen s to-boi ras-stat'-sia,   Te-bia mne bol'-she ne vi-

CHORUS

gain.   Dark the night _____ is;   Oh, I long for sleep!
дать.   Тем-на но-___-чень-ка!   Эх, да не спит-ся!
dat'.   Tem-na no-___-chen'-ka!   Ekh, da ne spit-sia!

2. Well I know the reason why
You and only you, my dear,
Come to me in every moment
And taunt my mind, that knows
    no rest.
    (Chorus)

2. Сам я знаю, почему
Ты, девчёночка, меня...
Ты одна меня тревожишь.
Одна решила мой спокой.
    (Chorus)

2. *Sam ia znaiu, pochemu*
Ty, devchënochka, menia . . .
Ty odna menia trevozhish'.
Odna reshila moi spokoi.
    (Chorus)

3. Once in May, do you recall
How we swam, just you and I?
Then upon the beach we rested;
How yellow was the sun-baked sand.
    (Chorus)

3. Вспомни, вспомни майский
    день!
Мы купаться с милой шли.
Мы садились на песочек.
На жёлтый, на мелкой песок.
    (Chorus)

3. *Vspomni, vspomni maiskii den'*
My kupat'sia s miloi shli.
My sadilis' na pesochek.
Na zhëltyi, na melkoi pesok.
    (Chorus)

THE LITTLE BELL

ОДНОЗВУЧНО ГРЕМИТ КОЛОКОЛЬЧИК

words by I. MAKAROV

Calmly

Oh, mo - not - o -nous -ly rings the
Од- но- звуч -но гре- мит ко - ло-
Od - no -zvuch -no gre -mit ko - lo-

coach bell, ___ And how dust -y the road that we
коль - чик, ___ И до - ро - га пы - лит - ся слег -
kol' - chik, ___ I do - ro - ga py - lit - sia sleg -

go. ___ Ring - ing sor - row -f'lly out o'er the high -way, ___ Pours the
ка. ___ И у - ны -ло по ров -но -му по - лю, ___ За -ли -
ka. ___ I u - ny - lo po rov -no -mu po - liu, ___ Za - li -

1.
coach-man his sad song of woe.
ва - ет -ся песнь ям -щи - ка.
va - et -sia pesn' iam -shchi - ka.

Final
road a -head runs out of sight. ___
мной да -ле -ка, да -ле - ка.
mnoi da - le - ka, da - le - ka.

2. How much feeling there is in that
     sad song,
   How much suffering in his refrain,
   That deep in my bosom it felt like
   My heart once again was aflame.

2. Сколько чувства в той песне
     унылой,
   Сколько грусти в напеве
     родном,
   Что в груди моей хладной,
     остылой
   Разгорелося сердце огнём.

2. *Skol'ko chuvstva v toi pesne unyloi,*
   Skol'ko grusti v napeve rodnom,
   Chto v grudi moei khladnoi, ostyloi
   Razgorelosia serdtse ognëm.

3. And it brought to my memory
     nights long past,
   Of the fields and the woods I hold
     dear,
   And from eyes that have long, long
     been dry,
   Like a jewel down my cheek rolled
     a tear.

3. И припомнил я ночи другие,
   И родные поля и леса,
   И на очи, давно уж сухие,
   Набежала, как искра, слеза.

3. *I pripomnil ia nochi drugie,*
   I rodnye polia i lesa,
   I na ochi, davno uzh sukhie,
   Nabezhala, kak iskra, sleza.

4. Oh, monotonously rings the coach
     bell,
   And it fades away far in the night.
   The coachman has now become
     silent.
   And the road ahead runs out of
     sight.

4. Однозвучно гремит
     колокольчик,
   Издали отдаваясь слегка,
   И замолк мой ямщик,
   А дорога предо мной далека,
     далека.

4. *Odnozvuchno gremit kolokol'chik,*
   Izdali otdavaias' slegka,
   I zamolk moi iamshchik,
   A doroga predo mnoi daleka,
     daleka.

Calmly, simply

Do not scold me and do not re-proach me,
Не ко-ри-те ме-ня, не бра-ни-те,
Ne ko-ri-te me-nia, ne bra-ni-te,

Not to love him was too much to ask.____ Hav-ing
не лю-бить я е-го не мог-ла.____ По-лю-
Ne liu-bit' ia e-vo ne mog-la.____ Po-liu-

DO NOT SCOLD ME AND DO NOT REPROACH ME

НЕ КОРИТЕ МЕНЯ,
НЕ БРАНИТЕ

fall - en in love, oh, so deep - ly, _____ Giv-ing all to him was my sweet task. _____
бив - ши же всё, что и - ме - ла, _____ Всё е - му я тог - да от - да - ла. _____
biv - shi zhe vsё, chto i - me - la, _____ Vsё e - mu ia tog - da ot - da - la. _____

---

2. Look and see what has now come upon me,
Where is my former beauty so rare,
And my cheeks that would outshine the sunrise,
And the thickness of my waving hair?

3. Where is my girlish, silver-bell laughter?
Where is my light-headed playfulness?
All to him, only him, and completely
Had I given in my recklessness.

4. I would like to forget my misfortune,
And forgive all the misdeeds of his.
Then don't scold me and do not reproach me,
Life is hard, hard enough as it is!

2. Посмотрите, что стало со мною,
Где былая моя красота?
Где румянец, что спорил с зарёю?
Где волнистых кудрей густота?

3. Где девичий мой смех серебристый,
Где беспечная резвость моя?
Всё ему одному безраздельно
Отдала, безрассудная я.

4. Я готова забыть своё горе
И простить ему всё его зло.
Не корите ж меня, не браните,
Мне и так тяжело, тяжело!

2. *Posmotrite, chto stalo so mnoiu,
Gde bylaia moia krasota?
Gde rumianets, chto sporil s zarёiu?
Gde volnistykh kudrei gustota?*

3. *Gde devichii moi smekh serebristyi,
Gde bespechnaia rezvost' moia?
Vsё emu odnomu bezrazdel'no
Otdala, bezrassudnaia ia.*

4. *Ia gotova zabyt' svoё gore
I prostit' emu vsё evo zlo.
Ne korite zh menia, ne branite,
Mne i tak tiazhelo, tiazhelo!*

NO SOUNDS FROM THE CITY ARE HEARD

НЕ СЛЫШНО ШУМУ ГОРОДСКОГО

2. Within, a poor young lad, a
   prisoner;
   A youth, a sapling in the spring,
   From his dark dungeon pours his
   sorrow.
   None but the river hears him sing.

3. "Forgive, forgive me, my dear
   fatherland,
   Forgive, my home, my family!
   For here, behind this iron grating
   I'm lost for an eternity.

4. "Forgive me, Father, and my
   sweetheart,
   Break up our wedding ring so fine.
   Be still, my heart, be still forever;
   A wife and children—never mine."

5. (*Repeat first verse*)

2. Вот бедный юноша, ровесник
   Младым, цветущим деревам,
   В глухой тюрьме заводит
   песню.
   И отдаёт тоску волнам.

3. «Прости, мой край, моя отчизна,
   Прости, мой дом, моя семья!
   Здесь, за решёткою железной,
   Навек от вас сокрылся я.

4. «Прости, отец, прости, невеста,
   Сломись, венчальное кольцо.
   Навек закройся, моё сердце,
   Не быть мне мужем и отцом.»

5. (Повторить первый куплет)

2. *Vot bednyi iunosha, rovesnik*
   Mladym, tsvetushchim derevam,
   V glukhoi tiur'me zavodit pesniu.
   I otdaët tosku volnam.

3. *"Prosti, moi krai, moia otchizna,*
   Prosti, moi dom, moia sem'ia!
   Zdes', za reshëtkoiu zheleznoi,
   Navek ot vas sokrylsia ia.

4. *"Prosti, otets, prosti, nevesta,*
   Slomis' venchal'noe kol'tso.
   Navek zakroisia, moë serdtse,
   Ne byt' mne muzhem i otsom."

5. (*Repeat first verse*)

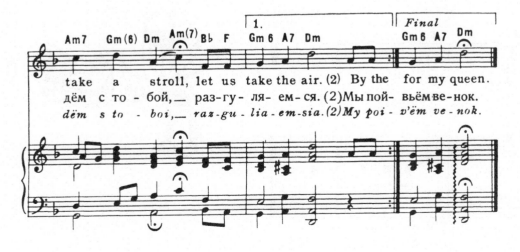

MY SWEETHEART

АХ ТЫ, ДУШЕЧКА

2. By the Volga's bank, strolling you and I,
   Walking side by side—let the hours fly.

3. Let the people look, let the people stare;
   Who's that couple yon?—What a lovely pair!

4. Sister, brother? No. Man and wife? Not so!
   That's two lovers there—anyone would know.

5. Hand-in-hand we'll go to the meadow green.
   Pretty flowers we'll pick—garlands for my queen.

2. Мы пойдём с тобой, разгуляемся,
   Вдоль по бережку Волги-матушки.

3. Эх, пускай на нас люди зарятся:
   «Ну и что ж это, что за парочка!

4. То не брат с сестрой, то не муж с женой,
   Добрый молодец с красной девицей!»

5. Мы пойдем с тобой в зеленой лужок,
   Мы нарвём цветов, мы совьём венок.

2. *My poidem s toboi, razguliaemsia,*
   Vdol' po berezhku Volgi-matushki.

3. *Ekh, puskai na nas liudi zariatsia:*
   "Nu i chto zh eto, chto za parochka!

4. *To ne brat s sestroi, to ne muzh s zhenoi,*
   Dobryi molodets s krasnoi devitsei!"

5. *My poidem s toboi v zelenoi luzhok,*
   My narvëm tsvetov, my sov'ëm venok.

With bounce

All through-out the great wide world I wan - dered,
Всю - то я все - лен - ну - ю про - е - хал,
Vsiu - to ia vse - len - nu - iu pro - e - khal,

True love was no-where to be found. heart.
Ни - где я ми - лой не на - шёл. -вет
Ni - gde ia mi - loi ne na - shël. vet.

ALL THROUGHOUT THE GREAT WIDE WORLD I WANDERED

ВСЮ-ТО Я ВСЕЛЕННУЮ ПРОЕХАЛ

2. Where are you, my radiant darling?
   Give me a token of your love.
   Oh, my pretty blue eyes, where are
       you,
   Where is the love that once I knew?

2. Где ж ты, светик, дорогая,
   Сердцу весточку подай,
   Где ж вы, очи голубые,
       Где ж ты, прежняя любовь?

2. *Gde zh ty, svetik, dorogaia,*
   Serdtsu vestochku podai,
   Gde zh vy, ochi golubye,
   Gde zh ty, prezhniaia liubov'?

3. Listen to the song I'm singing to
       you,
   Oh, my own, my dearest love.
   Turn your bright blue eyes once
       again to me,
   All the world shall be yours.

3. Ты заслышь мой голосочек,
   Разлюбезная моя,
       За твои за глазки голубые
       Всю вселенную отдам.

3. *Ty zaslysh' moi golosochek,*
   Razliubeznaia moia,
   Za tvoi za glazki golubye
   Vsiu vselennuiu otdam.

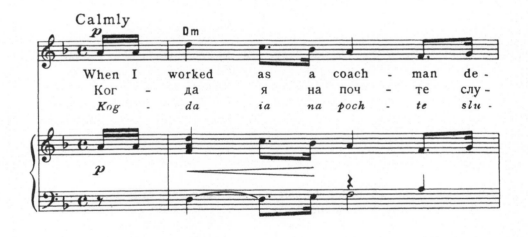

THE STORY
OF THE COACHMAN

РАССКАЗ ЯМЩИКА

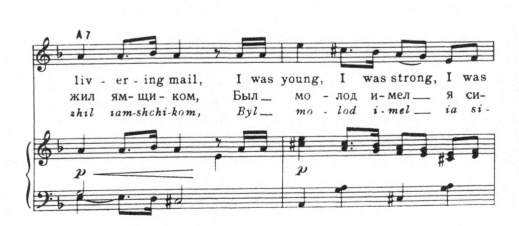

Calmly

When I worked as a coach - man de -
Ког - да я на поч - те слу -
Kog - da ia na poch - te slu -

liv - er - ing mail, I was young, I was strong, I was
жил ям - щи - ком, Был мо - лод и - мел я си -
zhil iam-shchi-kom, Byl mo - lod i-mel ia si -

heart - - - y. And be - lieve me, my boys, as I
лён - - ку, И креп - ко же, брат - цы, в се -
lën - - ku, I krep - ko zhe, brat - sy, v se -

tell you my tale, I loved dear - ly a cer - tain young par - ty.
ле - нье од - ном Лю - бил я в ту по - ру дев - чон - ку.
le - n'e od - nom, Liu - bil ia v tu po - ru dev - chon - ku.

2. Well, at first I could see nothing wrong loving her,
But my poor head, she started to spin it.
And wherever I'd travel, wherever I'd go,
To my darling I'd go for a minute.

2. Сначала не чуял я в девке беду,
Потом задурил не на шутку:
Куда ни поеду, куда ни пойду,
Всё к милой сверну на минутку.

2. *Snachala ne chuial ia v devke bedu,*
Potom zaduril ne na shutku:
Kuda ni poedu, kuda ni poidu,
Vsë k miloi svernu na minutku.

3. Love is sweet, so they say, but believe me, my friends,
There is no peace, with heartache and worry.
Once the chief said to me, as he gave me the mail,
"Here, deliver this package, and hurry!"

3. И любо оно, да покоя-то нет,
А сердце болит всё сильнее,
Однажды даёт мне начальник пакет:
«Свези, мол, на почту живее!»

3. *I liubo ono, da pokoia—to net,*
I serdtse bolit vsë sil'nee,
Odnazhdy daët mne nachal'nik paket:
"Svezi, mol, na pochtu zhivee!"

4. I took up the package and quickly to horse,
Like a fury o'er fields I soon started.
And deep in my breast my heart yearned and yearned,
As if we for a century were parted.

4. Я принял пакет — и скорей на коня,
И по полю вихрем помчался,
А сердце щемит да щемит у меня,
Как будто с ней век не видался.

4. *Ia prinial paket—i skorei na konia,*
I po poliu vikhrem pomchalsia,
A serdtse shchemit da shchemit u menia,
Kak budto s nei vek ne vidalsia.

5. And what was the reason—I can't understand—
   While the wail of the wind ever heightened,
   My horse, as if stricken, stopped dead in his tracks,
   And looked to the side as if frightened.

5. И что за причина — понять не могу,
   И ветер поёт так тоскливо . . .
   И вдруг словно замер мой конь на бегу,
   И в сторону смотрит пугливо.

5. *I chto za prichina—poniat' ne mogu,*
   I veter poët tak tosklivo . . .
   I vdrug slovno zamer moi kon' na begu,
   I v storonu smotrit puglivo.

6. My heart started pounding away in my breast,
   As I in alarm looked around.
   Then I sprang from the saddle of my trusty horse
   And I saw there a corpse on the ground.

6. Забилося сердце сильней у меня,
   И глянул вперёд я в тревоге,
   Потом соскочил с удалого коня,
   И вижу я труп на дороге.

6. *Zabilosia serdtse sil'nei u menia,*
   I glianul vperëd ia v trevoge,
   Potom soskochil s udalovo konia,
   I vizhu ia trup na doroge.

7. The snow almost covered up our rare find,
   As it swirled and it danced all around it.
   I dug up the drift and I froze to the spot—
   Oh, how I wish I never had found it.

7. А снег уж совсем ту находку занёс,
   Метель так и пляшет над трупом,
   Разрыл я сугроб-то и к месту прирос,
   Мороз заходил под тулупом.

7. *A sneg uzh sovsem tu nakhodku zanës,*
   Metel' tak i pliashet nad trupom,
   Razryl ia sugrob-to i k mestu priros,
   Moroz zakhodil pod tulupom.

8. For there in the snowdrifts lay this love of mine,
   Her eyes closed and her dear soul in Glory.
   Quick, pour me a glass of your sparkling red wine—
   I cannot continue my story.

8. Под снегом-то, братцы, лежала она . . .
   Закрылися карие очи.
   Налейте, налейте, скорее вина,
   Рассказывать больше нет мочи!

8. *Pod snegom—to, bratsy, lezhala ona . . .*
   Zakrylisia karie ochi.
   Naleite, naleite, skoree vina,
   Rasskazyvat' bol'she net mochi!

IN THE MEADOW STOOD A LITTLE BIRCH TREE

ВО ПОЛЕ БЕРЕЗЫНЬКА СТОЯЛА

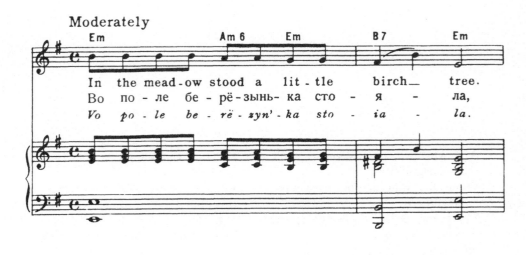

Moderately

In the mead-ow stood a lit-tle birch tree.
Во по - ле бе - рё - зынь - ка сто - я - ла,
Vo po - le be - rë - zyn' - ka sto - ia - la.

In the mead-ow stood a leaf-y birch tree.
Во по - ле куд - ря - ва - я сто - я - ла.
Vo po - le kud - ria - va - ia sto - ia - la.

Liu - li, liu - li a birch tree; Liu - li, liu - li a
Лю - ли, лю - ли, сто - я - ла, Лю - ли, лю - ли, сто -
Liu - li, liu - li sto - ia - la, Liu - li, liu - li sto -

CHORUS *(getting faster)*

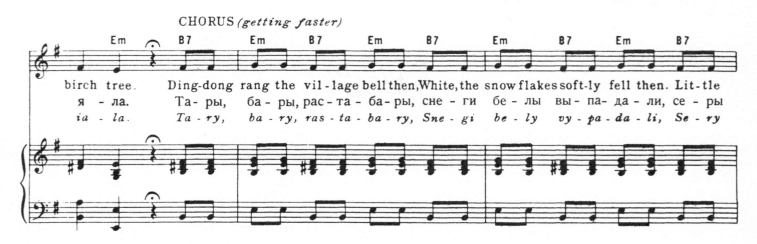

birch tree. Ding-dong rang the vil-lage bell then, White, the snow flakes soft-ly fell then. Lit-tle
я - ла. Та - ры, ба - ры, рас - та - ба - ры, сне - ги бе - лы вы - па - да - ли, се - ры
ia - la. Ta - ry, ba - ry, ras - ta - ba - ry, Sne - gi be - ly vy - pa - da - li, Se - ry

did - dle, did - dle, oh! What a mar - vel - lous oc - cur - rence, I was
На - виль, виль, виль, виль, Е - щё чу - до, пер - во чу - до, Чу - до
Na - vil', vil', vil', vil'. E - shchë chu - do, per - vo chu - do, Chu - do

1.
there, I saw it all. What a
ро - ди - на мо - я. Е - щё
ro - di - na mo - ia. E - shchë

2.
there, I saw it all.
ро - ди - на мо - я.
ro - di - na mo - ia.

2. No one put an ax to the birch tree.
No one harmed the little leafy birch
tree.
    Liuli, liuli, the birch tree;
    Liuli, liuli, the birch tree.
       (Chorus)

3. In the woods today I am going,
All to end the silver birch tree's
growing.
    Liuli, liuli, I'm going;
    Liuli, liuli, end its growing.
       (Chorus)

2. Некому берёзу заломати,
Некому кудряву защипати,
Люли, люли, заломати,
Люли, люли, защипати.
    (Chorus)

3. Пойду я в лес погуляю,
Белую берёзу заломаю,
Люли, люли, погуляю,
Люли, люли, заломаю.
    (Chorus)

2. *Nekomu berëzu zalomati,*
Nekomu kudriavu zashchipati,
Liuli, liuli, zalomati,
Liuli, liuli, zashchipati.
    (Chorus)

3. *Poidu ia v les poguliaiu,*
Beluiu berëzu zalomaiu,
Liuli, liuli, poguliaiu,
Liuli, liuli, zalomaiu.
    (Chorus)

THE BOUNDLESS
EXPANSE
OF THE SEA

РАСКИНУЛОСЬ МОРЕ
ШИРОКО

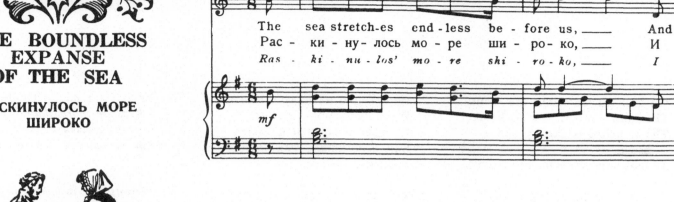

The sea stretch-es end-less be-fore us, ___ And
Рас - ки - ну - лось мо - ре ши - ро - ко, ___ И
Ras - ki - nu - los' mo - re shi - ro - ko, ___ I

waves rock the ship to and fro. ___ My
вол - ны бу - шу - ют вда - ли. ___ То -
vol - ny bu - shu - iut vda - li. ___ To -

friends, we are on a long jour - ney, Far from our dear land we must go, ___ My
ва - рищ, мы е - дем да - лё - ко, По - даль - ше от на - шей зем - ли. ___ То -
va - rishch, my e - dem da - lё - ko, Po - dal' she ot na - shei zem - li, ___ To -

friends, we are on a long jour - ney, Far from our dear land we must go.
ва - рищ, мы е - дем да - лё - ко, По - даль - ше от на - шей зем - ли.
va - rishch, my e - dem da - lё - ko, Po - dal' she ot na - shei zem - li.

2. On deck all the sailors are silent,
   The stormy waves over us break.
   The shoreline is gloomy and
   dismal,
   To look at it makes the heart ache.

3. "I cannot continue my labor,"
   One stoker he said to the other.
   "My furnace will soon be all
   burned out,
   I can't keep the steam up, my
   brother."

4. "Please go and report to the doctor
   That I'm sick," the stoker said,
   sighing.
   "I'm faint from the heat of the
   furnace,
   My strength is all gone, I am
   dying."

5. The friend left—he picked up his
   shovel,
   And dragging himself to his feet,
   Kicked open the door of the
   furnace
   And faced once again the cruel
   heat.

6. On finishing stoking he drank
   deep
   Of water—distilled but unclear.
   The sooty sweat dripped from his
   forehead,
   When up spoke the chief engineer.

7. "You, stoker, your watch isn't
   finished,
   You haven't completed your trick.
   Get up to the doctor this minute,
   He'll cure you if you're really
   sick!"

---

2. Не слышно на палубе песен,
   И Красное море шумит,
   И берег и мрачен и тесен,
   Как вспомнишь, так сердце
   болит.

3. «Товарищ, я вахты не в силах
   стоять,»
   Сказал кочегар кочегару,
   «Огни в моих топках совсем
   прогорят,
   В котлах не сдержать мне уж
   пару.

4. «Пойди, заяви, что я заболел
   И вахту, не кончив, бросаю.
   Весь потом истёк, от жары
   изнемог,
   Работать нет сил, умираю!»

5. Товарищ ушёл . . . Лопатку
   схватил,
   Собравши последние силы,
   Дверь топки привычным
   толчком отворил,
   И пламя его озарило.

6. Окончив кидать, он напился
   воды,
   Воды опреснённой, нечистой,
   С лица его падал пот, сажи
   следы . . .
   Услышал он речь машиниста:

7. «Ты вахты, не кончив, не
   смеешь бросать,
   Механик тобой недоволен;
   Ты к доктору должен пойти
   и сказать,
   Лекарство он даст, если
   болен!»

---

2. *Ne slyshno na palube pesen,*
   I Krasnoe more shumit,
   I bereg i mrachen i tesen,
   Kak vspomnish', tak serdtse bolit.

3. *"Tovarishch, ia vakhty ne v silakh*
   stoiat',"
   Skazal kochegar kochegaru,
   "Ogni v moikh topkakh sovsem
   progoriat,
   V kotlakh ne sderzhat' mne uzh
   paru.

4. *"Poidi, zaiavi, chto ia zabolel*
   I vakhtu, ne konchiv, brosaiu.
   Ves' potom istëk, ot zhary
   iznemog,
   Rabotat' net sil, umiraiu!"

5. *Tovarishch ushël . . . Lopatku*
   skhvatil,
   Sobravshi poslednie sily,
   Dver' topki privychnym tolchkom
   otvoril,
   I plamia evo ozarilo.

6. *Okonchiv kidat', on napilsia vody,*
   Vody opresnënnoi, nechistoi,
   S litsa evo padal pot, sazhi
   sledy . . .
   Uslyshal on rech' mashinista:

7. *"Ty vakhty, ne konchiv, ne*
   smeesh' brosat',
   Mekhanik toboi nedovolen;
   Ty k doktoru dolzhen poiti i
   skazat',
   Lekarstvo on dast, esli bolen!"

8. He stumbled on deck in a stupor,
   His eyes rolled—he saw not at all.
   Then came for an instant a bright
   flash,
   And down on the deck he did fall.

8. На палубу вышел . . . Сознанья
   уж нет.
   В глазах его всё
   помутилось . . .
   Увидел на миг ослепительный
   свет . . .
   Упал . . . Сердце больше не
   билось . . .

8. *Na palubu vyshel . . . Soznan'ia*
   uzh net.
   V glazakh evo vsë pomutilos' . . .
   Uvidel na mig oslepitel'nyi svet . . .
   Upal . . . Serdtse bol'she ne
   bilos' . . .

9. Next morning his friends bade him
   farewell,
   The sailors who knew this poor
   stoker,
   And buried him in the wide ocean
   Together with his rusty poker.

9. Проститься с товарищем
   утром пришли
   Матросы, друзья кочегара,
   Последний подарок ему
   поднесли —
   Колосник горелый и ржавый.

9. *Prostit'sia s tovarishchem utrom*
   prishli
   Matrosy, druz'ia kochegara,
   Poslednii podarok emu podnesli—
   Kolosnik gorelyi i rzhavyi.

10. In vain does his mother await him;
    She'll know soon enough, never
    fear.
    From stem to the stern the cruel
    waves rush on,
    And gradually disappear.

10. Напрасно старушка ждёт сына
    домой,
    Ей скажут, она зарыдает . . .
    А волны бегут от винта за
    кормой,
    И след их вдали пропадает.

10. *Naprasno starushka zhdët syna*
    domoi,
    Ei skazhut, ona zarydaet . . .
    A volny begut ot vinta za kormoi,
    I sled ikh vdali propadaet.

On the Vol - ga's a cliff, with wild
Есть на Вол - ге у - тёс, ди - ким
Est' na Vol - ge u - tës, di - kim

THE CLIFF
ON THE VOLGA

УТЕС

moss o - ver - grown From its foot to its high, loft - y
мо - хом об - рос Он с вер - ши - ны до са - мо - го
mo - khom ob - ros On s ver - shi - ny do sa - mo - vo

words by A. NAVROTSKY

2. Its summit is bare, no life blossoms
   there,
   Just the wild wind whips fiercely;
   and glowers
   The proud eagle, whose cries echo
   up to the skies,
   As its prey in its nest it devours.

3. Of brave men, only one ever
   climbed to the top,
   To its summit, so high and wind-
   blown.
   Well remembers the cliff this brave
   visitor's climb,
   And from that day by his name 'tis
   well known.

4. Many thoughts came to him as he
   stood on that cliff,
   Many thoughts—only he was to
   know them.
   O'er the murmuring waves in the
   stillness of night
   He conceived daring deeds—he
   would show them!

5. And to this day the cliff, like a
   sentinel, guards
   All the secrets and dreams of
   Stepan.
   With the Volga alone does it share
   memories
   Of the valiant life of the brave
   chieftain.

2. На вершине его не растёт
   ничего,
   Только ветер свободный гуляет,
   Да могучий орёл свой притон
   там завёл
   И на нём свои жертвы терзает.

3. Из людей лишь один на утёсе
   том был,
   Лишь один до вершины
   добрался.
   И утёс человека того не забыл
   И с тех пор его именем
   звался . . .

4. Много дум в голове родилось
   у него,
   Много дум он в ту ночь
   передумал,
   И под говор волны, средь
   ночной тишины,
   Он великое дело задумал.

5. И поныне стоит тот утёс и
   хранит
   Все заветные думы Степана,
   И лишь с Волгой одной
   вспоминает порой
   Удалое житьё атамана.

2. *Na vershine evo ne rastët nichevo,*
   Tol'ko veter svobodnyi guliaet,
   Da moguchii orël svoi priton tam
   zavël
   I na nëm svoi zhertvy terzaet.

3. *Iz liudei lish' odin na utëse tom byl,*
   Lish' odin do vershiny dobralsia.
   I utës cheloveka tovo ne zabyl
   I s tekh por evo imenem zvalsia . . .

4. *Mnogo dum v golove rodilos' u*
   nevo,
   Mnogo dum on v tu noch'
   peredumal,
   I pod govor volny, sred' nochnoi
   tishiny,
   On velikoe delo zadumal.

5. *I ponyne stoit tot utës i khranit*
   Vse zavetnye dumy Stepana,
   I lish' s Volgoi odnoi vspominaet
   poroi
   Udaloe zhit'ë atamana.

SNOW FLURRIES

ВДОЛЬ ПО УЛИЦЕ
МЕТЕЛИЦА МЕТЕТ

music by A. VARLAMOV

Moderately

Down the vil-lage street the snow storm swirls and blows,
Вдоль по у-ли-це ме-те-ли-ца ме-тёт,
Vdol' po u-li-tse me-te-li-tsa me-tët,

Through the snow storm there I see my dar-ling goes.
За ме-те-ли-цей мой ми-лень-кий и-дёт.
Za me-te-li-tsei moi mi-len'-kii i-dët.

Stay a-while, oh, stay and turn your face to mine. Let me gaze up
Ты по-стой, по-стой, кра-са-ви-ца мо-я, До-зволь на-гля-
Ty po-stoi, po-stoi, kra-sa-vi-tsa mo-ia, Do-zvol' na-glia-

1.
on you, see your beau-ty shine.
деть-ся, ра-дость, на те-бя.
det'-sia, ra-dost', na te-bia.

2.
see your beau-ty shine.
ра-дость на те-бя.
ra-dost', na te-bia.

2. Oh, your beauty and your most
    exquisite grace;
  Dark your lovely eyes and lily-white
    your face.
    (*Chorus*)

2. На твою ли на приятну
    красоту,
  На твое ли, что ль на белое
    лицо.
    (*Chorus*)

2. *Na tvoiu li na priiatnu krasotu,*
  Na tvoë li, chto l' na beloe litso.
  (*Chorus*)

3. Oh, your beauty has caused me to
    pine and sigh,
  And to waste away, such a brave
    young lad as I.
    (*Chorus*)

3. Красота твоя с ума меня свела.
  Иссушила добра молодца меня.
  (*Chorus*)

3. *Krasota tvoia s uma menia svela,*
  Issushila dobra molodtsa menia.
  (*Chorus*)

STENKA RAZIN (FROM BEYOND THE ISLAND)

ИЗ-ЗА ОСТРОВА НА СТРЕЖЕНЬ (Стенька Разин)

'Round the
Из - за
Iz - za

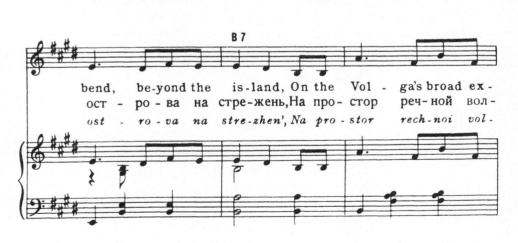

bend, be-yond the is-land, On the Vol - ga's broad ex-
ост - ро - ва на стре-жень, На про-стор реч-ной вол-
ost - ro - va na stre-zhen', Na pro-stor rech-noi vol-

panse, Bright-ly paint-ed, man-y col-ored, sharp-ly breast-ed barques ad-
ны, Вы-плы-ва-ют рас-пис-ны-е, ост-ро-гру-ды-е чел-
ny, Vy-ply-va-iut ras-pis-ny-e, ost-ro-gru-dy-e chel-

vance. Bright-ly paint-ed, man-y col-ored, sharp-ly breast-ed barques ad-vance.
ны. Вы-плы-ва-ют рас-пис-ны-е, ост-ро-гру-ды-е чел-ны.
ny. Vy-ply-va-iut ras-pis-ny-e, ost-ro-gru-dy-e chel-ny.

2. On the lead-ship, *Stenka Razin,*
   With his princess sits all day.
   A new wedding celebrating,
   He is tipsy, he is gay.

3. All around the crew is grumbling:
   "He forsook us for this girl.
   Just one night with her he dallied,
   Now his head is in a whirl."

4. All the slander and derision
   By the chieftain it was heard.
   Held his Persian princess tightly,
   But within him anger stirred.

2. На переднем Стенька Разин,
   Обнявшись сидит с княжной,
   Свадьбу новую справляет
   Он весёлый и хмельной.

3. Позади их слышен ропот:
   «Нас на бабу променял,
   Только ночь с ней провожжался,
   Сам на утро бабой стал.»

4. Этот ропот и насмешки
   Слышит грозный атаман,
   И могучею рукою
   Обнял персиянки стан.

2. *Na perednem Sten'ka Razin,*
   Obniavshis' sidit s kniazhnoi,
   Svad'bu novuiu spravliaet
   On vesëlyi i khmel'noi.

3. *Pozadi ikh slyshen ropot:*
   "Nas na babu promenial,
   Tol'ko noch' s nei provozhalsia,
   Sam na utro baboi stal."

4. *Etot ropot i nasmeshki*
   Slyshit groznyi ataman,
   I mogucheiu rukoiu
   Obnial persiianki stan.

5. To his eyes the blood rushed
   fiercely,
   To the chieftain's fiery eyes.
   With mad rage his brows
   contracted,
   From his lips poured forth wild
   cries:

6. "There's no deed can make me
   tremble;
   Proudly I will give my head."
   To the distance his voice
   thundered,
   The shores heard the words he
   said.

7. "Volga, Volga, Mother Volga,
   Volga, Volga, river great,
   A Don Cossack sacrifices,
   And I will not hesitate!

8. "That there should be no
   dissension
   'Mongst my men so brave and
   free,
   Volga, Volga, Mother Volga,
   Here, accept this gift from me!"

9. With a mighty swoop he raises
   Up on high the Persian maid;
   Overboard he swiftly casts her,
   In a watery grave she's laid.

10. "Hey there, boys, why are you
    downcast?
    Dance, there! Filka—encore, bis!
    Strike a song, a stirring fast one—
    May her poor soul rest in peace!"

5. Алой кровью налилися
   Атамановы глаза,
   Брови чёрные сошлися,
   Надвигается гроза.

6. «Ничего не пожалею,
   Буйну голову отдам!»
   Раздаётся голос властный,
   По окрестным берегам.

7. «Волга, Волга, мать родная,
   Волга, русская река,
   Не видала ты подарка
   От донского казака!

8. «Чтобы не было раздора
   Между вольными людьми,
   Волга, Волга, мать родная,
   На, красавицу прими!»

9. Мощным взмахом поднимает
   Он красавицу-княжну
   И за борт её бросает
   В набежавшую волну.

10. «Что ж вы, братцы, приуныли?
    Эй, ты, Филька, чорт, пляши!
    Грянем песню удалую
    На помин её души!»

5. *Aloi krov'iu nalilisia*
   Atamanovy glaza,
   Brovi chërnye soshlisia,
   Nadvigaetsia groza.

6. *"Nichevo ne pozhaleiu,*
   Buinu golovu otdam!"
   Razdaëtsia golos vlastnyi,
   Po okrestnym beregam.

7. *"Volga, Volga, mat' rodnaia,*
   Volga, russkaia reka,
   Ne vidala ty podarka
   Ot donskovo kazaka!

8. *"Chtoby ne bylo razdora*
   Mezhdu vol'nymi liud'mi,
   Volga, Volga, mat' rodnaia,
   Na, krasavitsu primi!"

9. *Moshchnym vzmakhom podnimaet*
   On krasavitsu-kniazhnu
   I za bort eë brosaet
   V nabezhavshuiu volnu.

10. *"Chto zh vy, bratsy, priunyli?*
    Ei, ty, Fil'ka, chort, pliashi!
    Grianem pesniu udaluiu
    Na pomin eë dushi!"

TROIKA RUSHING

ТРОЙКА МЧИТСЯ

words by P. VYAZEMSKY
music by P. BULAKHOV

Lively

Troi - ka rush - ing,
Трой - ка мчит - ся,
Troi - ka mchit - sia,

troi - ka dash - ing, Dust is ris - ing from the ground.
трой - ка ска - чет, Вьёт - ся пыль из - под ко - пыт.
troi - ka ska - chet, V'ët - sia pyl' iz - pod ko - pyt.

Lit - tle bell is laugh - ing, ring - ing. Troi - ka, tell_ me, where you're bound._
Ко - ло - коль - чик звон - ко пла - чет, и хо - хо - чет, и зве - нит.___
Ko - lo - kol'-chik zvon - ko pla - chet, i kho - kho - chet, i zve - nit.___

CHORUS *(faster)*   *a little slower*

Rid - ing, rid - ing, rid - ing fast, See my own true love at last.
Е - ду, е - ду, е - ду к ней, Е - ду к лю - буш - ке мо - ей.
E - du, e - du, e - du k nei, E - du k liu - bush - ke mo - ei.

Riding, riding, riding fast, See my own true love at last.
Е - ду, е - ду, е - ду к ней, Е - ду к лю - буш - ке мо - ей.
E - du, e - du, e - du k nei, E - du k liu - bush - ke mo - ei.

2. Who is riding on the troika,
   Whence comes he and whither
     bound,
   Willy nilly speeding onward,
   With the darkness all around?
   (*Chorus*)

3. How to know?—he's sped right
     by us,
   And the moon's behind a cloud.
   In the far-off empty distance
   Still the bell that rang so loud.
   (*Chorus*)

2. Кто сей путник и отколе?
   И далёк ли путь ему?
   Поневоле иль по воле
   Мчится он в ночную тьму?
   (*Chorus*)

3. Как узнать? Уж он далёко.
   Месяц в облако нырнул
   И в пустой дали глубокой
   Колокольчик уж заснул.
   (*Chorus*)

2. *Kto sei putnik i otkole?*
   I dalëk li put' emu?
   Ponevole il' po vole
   Mchitsia on v nochnuiu t'mu?
   (*Chorus*)

3. *Kak uznat'? Uzh on dalëko.*
   Mesiats v oblako nyrnul
   I v pustoi dali glubokoi
   Kolokol'chik uzh zasnul.
   (*Chorus*)

My mem-o-ries do not a-wak-en
Не про-буж-дай вос-по-ми-на-нья
Ne pro-buzh-dai vos-po-mi-na-n'ia

DO NOT AWAKEN MY MEMORIES

НЕ ПРОБУЖДАИ ВОСПОМИНАНЬЯ

Of days gone by, of days gone by.
Ми-нув-ших дней, ми-нув-ших дней.
Mi-nuv-shikh dnei, mi-nuv-shikh dnei.

music by P. BULAKHOV

2. Don't cast your fateful glances on me;
Your wicked eyes, your wicked eyes.
Don't tempt me now with words of honey,
With empty lies, with empty lies.

2. И на меня свой взор опасный
Не устремляй, не устремляй;
Мечтой любви, мечтой прекрасной
Не увлекай, не увлекай!

2. *I na menia svoi vzor opasnyi*
Ne ustremliai, ne ustremliai;
Mechtoi liubvi, mechtoi prekrasnoi
Ne uvlekai, ne uvlekai!

3. When happiness comes, grasp it
      tightly,
   Be thankful then, be thankful then.
   And when the fire of love burns
      brightly
   We live again, we live again.

4. You who put out that sacred fire,
   Oh, let it burn, oh, let it burn.
   Those precious hours of love's
      desire
   Will ne'er return, will ne'er return.

3. Однажды счастье в жизни
      этой
   Вкушаем мы, вкушаем мы,
   Святым огнём любви согреты,
   Оживлены, оживлены.

4. Но кто её огонь священный
   Мог погасить, мог погасить,
   Тому уж жизни незабвенной
   Не возвратить, не возвратить!

3. *Odnazhdy schast'e v zhizni etoi*
   Vkushaem my, vkushaem my,
   Sviatym ognëm liubvi sogrety,
   Ozhivleny, ozhivleny.

4. *No kto eë ogon' sviashchennyi*
   Mog pogasit', mog pogasit',
   Tomu uzh zhizni nezabvennoi
   Ne vozvratit', ne vozvratit'!

ALONG
THE PETERSKAYA
ROAD

ВДОЛЬ ПО ПИТЕРСКОЙ

Hey! Down broad Pe-ter-skoy street.
Эх, вдоль по Пи-тер-ской,
Ekh, vdol' po Pi-ter-skoi,

Down Tver-ska-ya____ Yam-ska-ya street, I said,
По Твер-ской Ям-ской, да, ох, По Твер-
Po Tver-skoi Iam-skoi, da, okh,— Po Tver-

3. I was at a feast,
   At a gay party, hey!
   I did not drink mead,
   I drank sweet vodka, hey!

4. I drank sweet vodka,
   And I also drank brandy, hey!
   And I drank (oh, you kid)
   From a half a pail.

Note: Verse 3 is sung to melody of
Verse 2; Verse 4 is sung to
melody of Verse 1.

IN THE VALLEY

СРЕДИ ДОЛИНЫ РОВНЫЕ

words by A. MERZLIAKOV

Moderately

Out in the val-ley,
Сре-ди до-ли-ны
Sre-di do-li-ny

on the plain, Up-on the lev-el plain,___ There
ров-ны-я, На глад-кой вы-со-те___ Цве-
rov-ny-ia, Na glad-koi vy-so-te___ Tsve-

grows an oak, a might-y oak Of a___ ma-jes-tic mien. There
тёт, рас-тёт___ вы-со-кий дуб В мо-гу-чей кра-со-те. Цве-
tёt, ras-tёt vy-so-kii dub V mo-gu-chei kra-so-te. Tsve-

grows an oak,___ a might-y oak, Of a___ ma-jes-tic mien.
тёт, рас-тёт___ вы-со-кий дуб В мо-гу-чей кра-со-те.
tёt, ras-tёt___ vy-so-kii dub V mo-gu-chei kra-so-te.

2. A mighty oak, a spreading oak,
   A beauty to regard.
   Alone, alone, how pitiful,
   A sentry standing guard.

3. And when the summer sun burns
   hot,
   None seeks its welcome shade.
   And when the wintry storms rage
   fierce,
   It stands alone, afraid.

4. No curly pine trees grow nearby,
   No willow waves its head.
   No leaf of green, no blade of grass,
   All life around has fled.

5. How sad it is to live alone,
   How sad e'en for a tree.
   How bitter, bitter for a man
   Without his love to be.

6. Much silver have I, and much
   gold,
   Upon whom to bestow?
   There is much fame and honor
   rare;
   With whom, then, shall I go?

7. There are some men whom I
   avoid,
   Still others stay away.
   They all are friends, fair-weather
   friends;
   Until a rainy day.

8. Where, then, to rest my weary
   heart
   When storms around me sweep?
   My dearest one can't help me now,
   He (she) in the ground does sleep.

2. Высокий дуб, развесистый,
   Один у всех в глазах;
   Один, один, бедняжечка,
   Как рекрут на часах!

3. Взойдёт ли красно солнышко,
   Кого под тень принять?
   Ударит ли погодушка,
   Кто будет защищать?

4. Ни сосенки кудрявые,
   Ни ивки близ него,
   Ни кустики зелёные
   Не вьются вкруг него.

5. Ах, скучно одинокому
   И дереву расти!
   Ах, горько, горько молодцу
   Без милой жизнь вести.

6. Есть много сребра, золота,
   Кого им подарить?
   Есть много славы, почестей,
   Но с кем их разделить?

7. Одних я сам чуждаюся,
   Другой бежит меня,
   Все други, все приятели
   До чёрного лишь дня.

8. Где ж сердцем отдохнуть
   могу,
   Когда гроза взойдёт?
   Друг нежный спит в сырой
   земле,
   На помощь не придёт.

2. *Vysokii dub, razvesistyi,*
   Odin u vsekh v glazakh;
   Odin, odin, bedniazhechka,
   Kak rekrut na chasakh!

3. *Vzoidët li krasno solnyshko,*
   Kovo pod ten' priniat'?
   Udarit li pogodushka,
   Kto budet zashchishchat'?

4. *Ni sosenki kudriavye,*
   Ni ivki bliz nevo,
   Ni kustiki zelënye
   Ne v'iutsia vkrug nevo.

5. *Akh, skuchno odinokomu*
   I derevu rasti!
   Akh, gor'ko, gor'ko molodtsu
   Bes miloi zhizn' vesti.

6. *Est' mnogo srebra, zolota,*
   Kovo im podarit'?
   Est' mnogo slavy, pochestei,
   No s kem ikh razdelit?

7. *Odnikh ia sam chuzhdaiusia,*
   Drugoi bezhit menia,
   Vse drugi, vse priiateli
   Do chërnovo lish' dnia.

8. *Gde zh serdtsem otdokhnut' mogu,*
   Kogda groza vzoidët?
   Drug nezhnyi spit v syroi zemle,
   Na pomoshch' ne pridët.

9. No kin have I, nor family,
   All in this foreign land.
   Nor have I a dear sweetheart
   To take me by the hand.

10. Nor shall they ever weep for joy,
    The old folks tenderly.
    No little ones around us play,
    All that was not to be.

11. Take back, take back, then, all
    your gold;
    Your honors, too, likewise,
    And give me back my home, my
    love,
    One glance from my love's eyes.

9. Ни роду нет, ни племени
   В чужой мне стороне;
   Не ластится любезная
   Подруженька ко мне.

10. Не плачется от радости
    Старик, глядя на нас;
    Не вьются вкруг малюточки,
    Тихохонько резвясь.

11. Возьмите же всё золото,
    Все почести назад,
    Мне родину, мне милую,
    Мне милой дайте взгляд!

9. *Ni rodu net, ni plemeni*
   V chuzhoi mne storone;
   Ne lastitsia liubeznaia
   Podruzhen'ka ko mne.

10. *Ne plachetsia ot radosti*
    Starik, gliadia na nas;
    Ne v'iutsia vkrug maliutochki,
    Tikhokhon'ko rezvias'.

11. *Voz'mite zhe vsë zoloto,*
    Vse pochesti nazad,
    Mne rodinu, mne miluiu,
    Mne miloi daite vzgliad!

Moderately

Here on the road we pass a vil-lage, My coach-man
Вот на пу-ти се-ло боль-шо-е, Ку-да ям-
Vot na pu-ti se-lo bol'-sho-e, Ku-da iam-

turns and ga-zes_long. His ar-dent heart be-gins_ to
щик мой по-гля-дел, Е-го за-би-лось,ре-ти-
shchik moi po-glia-del, E-vo za-bi-los' re-ti-

THE VILLAGE
ON THE ROAD

ВОТ НА ПУТИ СЕЛО БОЛЬШОЕ

music by P. BULAKHOV

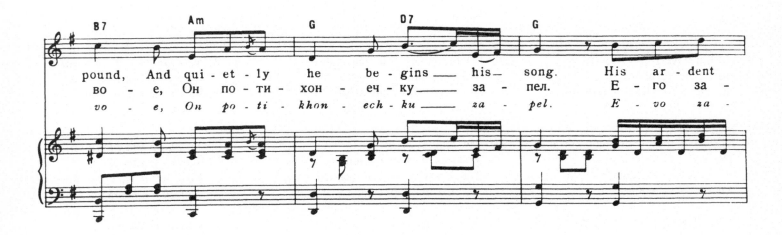

pound, And qui-et-ly he be-gins___ his___ song. His ar-dent
во - е, Он по-ти-хон - еч-ку___ за-пел. Е-го за-
vo - e, On po-ti - khon - ech-ku___ za - pel. E-vo za -

heart be-gins to pound, And qui-et-ly he be-gins___ his___ song.
би - лось ре-ти-во - е, он по-ти-хон - еч-ку___ за-пел.
bi - los' re - ti - vo - e, On po - ti - khon - ech-ku___ za - pel.

2. "I am held captive by your beauty,
   For me the sun and stars don't
      shine.
   Tell me, oh, why did you bewitch
      me
   If in your heart you were not mine?

3. "My trusty horses, they will miss
      me,
   Poor things, they've shared my
      heavy load.
   When I am gone they will not
      gallop
   Past the mileposts on the road.

4. "Not for long will I be singing,
   Just to amuse my riders here.
   Soon beneath the earth they'll lay
      me,
   None behind to shed a tear."

2. «Твоя краса меня прельстила,
   Теперь мне белый свет не мил,
   Зачем, скажи, приворожила,
   Коль я душе твоей немил.

3. По мне лошадушки сгрустнутся,
   Расставшись, бедные, со мной,
   Они уж больше не промчатся
   Вдоль по дороге столбовой.

4. Не долго песнью удалою,
   Не долго тешить седока,
   Уж скоро, скоро под землёю
   Зароют тело ямщика.»

2. *"Tvoia krasa menia prel'stila,*
   Teper' mne belyi svet ne mil,
   Zachem, skazhi, privorozhila,
   Kol' ia dushe tvoei nemil.

3. *Po mne loshadushki sgrustnutsia,*
   Rasstavshis', bednye, so mnoi,
   Oni uzh bol'she ne promchatsia
   Vdol' po doroge stolbovoi.

4. *Ne dolgo pesn'iu udaloiu,*
   Ne dolgo teshit' sedoka,
   Uzh skoro, skoro pod zemlëiu
   Zaroiut telo iamshchika."

KALINKA
(LITTLE
SNOWBALL BUSH)

КАЛИНКА

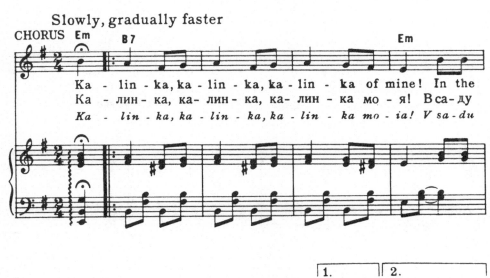

Slowly, gradually faster

CHORUS

Ka - lin - ka, ka - lin - ka, ka - lin - ka of mine! In the
Ка - лин - ка, ка - лин - ка, ка - лин - ка мо - я! В са - ду
Ka - lin - ka, ka - lin - ka, ka - lin - ka mo - ia! V sa - du

gar-den grows a ber - ry like sweet sher-ry wine. Ka - wine. Oh,
я - го - да ма - лин - ка, ма - лин - ка мо - я! Ка - я. Ах,
ia - go - da ma - lin - ka, ma - lin - ka mo - ia! Ka - ia. Akh,

Fine

Un - der the pine tree, un - der the green tree. There I'll
Под сос - но - ю, под зе - лё - но - ю, Спать по - ло -
Pod sos - no - iu, pod ze - lë - no - iu, Spat' po - lo -

lay me down to sleep. Ah! Ay, liu - li, liu - li, ay, liu -
жи - те вы ме - ня. А - Ай лю - ли, лю - ли, ай лю -
zhi - te vy me - nia. A - ai liu - li, liu - li, ai liu -

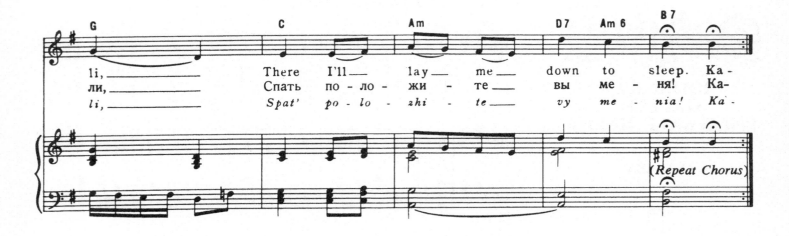

li, _____ There I'll __ lay __ me __ down to sleep. Ka-

ли, _____ Спать по-ло-жи-те __ вы ме-ня! Ka-

li, _____ Spat' po-lo-zhi-te __ vy me-nia! Ka-

(Repeat Chorus)

2. Little pine tree, thou evergreen tree,
   With your rustling do not wake me.
   Ay, liuli, liuli. Ay, liuli,
   With your rustling do not wake me.
   (*Repeat Chorus*)

3. Oh, my darling, lovely maiden,
   Won't you promise to be mine.
   Ay, liuli, liuli. Ay, liuli,
   Won't you promise to be mine.
   (*Repeat Chorus*)

2. Ах! Сосёнушка ты зелёная,
   Не шуми же надо мной!
   Ай-люли, люли, ай-люли,
   Не шуми же надо мной!
   (Повторить припев)

3. Ах! Красавица, душа-девица,
   Полюби же ты меня!
   Ай-люли, люли, ай-люли,
   Полюби же ты меня!
   (Повторить припев)

2. *Akh! Sosënushka ty zelënaia,*
   Ne shumi zhe nado mnoi!
   Ai—liuli, liuli, ai—liuli,
   Ne shumi zhe nado mnoi!
   (*Repeat Chorus*)

3. *Akh! Krasavitsa, dusha-devitsa,*
   Poliubi zhe ty menia!
   Ai—liuli, liuli, ai—liuli,
   Poliubi zhe ty menia!
   (*Repeat Chorus*)

Not fast, with expression

Why do
Что ты
Chto ty

you ea-ger-ly at the high-way Glance, and
жад-но гля-дишь на до-ро-гу, Всто-ро-
zhad no glia-dish' na do-ro- gu, Vsto-ro-

WHY DO YOU GAZE AT THE ROAD?

ЧТО ТЫ ЖАДНО ГЛЯДИШЬ НА ДОРОГУ

words by N. NEKRASOV

2. Tell me why do you run out so quickly
   As the troika goes galloping by?
   You were standing so prettily there
   That the traveler cast you his eye.

3. Just one glance from a raven-eyed charmer
   Is like witchcraft, inflaming the blood:
   An old man will bestow precious presents;
   In the young man's heart true love will flood.

2. И зачем ты бежишь торопливо
   За промчавшейся тройкой во след?
   На тебя, подбоченясь красиво,
   Загляделся проезжий корнет...

3. Взгляд один чернобровой дикарки,
   Полный чар, зажигающих кровь,
   Старика разорит на подарки,
   В сердце юноши кинет любовь.

2. *I zachem ty bezhish' toroplivo*
   Za promchavsheisia troikoi vo sled?
   Na tebia, podbochenias' krasivo,
   Zagliadelsia proezzhii kornet . . .

3. *Vzgliad odin chernobrovoi dikarki,*
   Polnyi char, zazhigaiushchikh krov',
   Starika razorit na podarki,
   V serdtse iunoshi kinet liubov'.

4. Better live for a while and be
      happy;
   If you try, life will be rich and gay.
   But that did not fall to your fortune,
   All too soon your black hair will
      turn gray.

5. And deep in a damp grave they'll
      lay you,
   When your life it has come to an
      end;
   Uselessly flickered-out lifetime,
   Lifetime without love or a friend.

6. So don't look at the road with such
      longing,
   As the troika goes by with a rush;
   And the painful heartache that's
      within you,
   Quickly, quickly, forever please
      hush.

4. Поживёшь и попразднуешь
      вволю,
   Будет жизнь и полна, и
      легка . . .
   — Да не то тебе пало на долю:
   За неряху пойдёшь мужика . . .

5. И схоронят в сырую могилу,
   Как пройдёшь ты тяжёлый свой
      путь,
   Бесполезно угасшую силу
   И ни чем не согретую грудь.

6. Не гляди же с тоской на дорогу
   И за тройкой во след не спеши.
   И тоскливую в сердце тревогу
   Поскорей навсегда заглуши! •

4. *Pozhivёsh' i poprazdnuesh' vvoliu,*
   Budet zhizn' i polna, i legka . . .
   Da ne to tebe palo na doliu:
   Za neriakhu poidёsh' muzhika . . .

5. *I skhoroniat v syruiu mogilu,*
   Kak proidёsh' ty tiazhёlyi svoi put',
   Bespolezno ugasshuiu silu
   I nichem ne sogretuiu grud'.

6. *Ne gliadi zhe s toskoi na dorogu*
   I za troikoi vo sled ne speshi.
   I tosklivuiu v serdtse trevogu
   Poskorei navsegda zaglushi!

SONG OF THE VOLGA BOATMEN

ЭЙ, УХНЕМ!

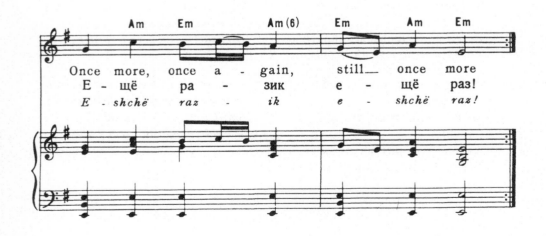

VERSE

2. (*Refrain*)
Verse:

As the barges float along,
To the sun we sing our song.
Ay-da, da, ay-da!
Ay-da, da, ay-da!
To the sun we sing our song.
Hey, hey, let's heave along the way,
To the sun we sing our song.

3. (*Refrain*)
Verse:

Volga, Volga our pride,
Mighty stream so deep and wide.
Ay-da, da, ay-da!
Ay-da, da, ay-da!
Mighty stream so deep and wide.
Hey, hey, that is why we say
Volga, Volga, you're our pride.

2. (*Refrain*)
Verse:

Мы по бережку идём,
Песню солнышку поём,
Ай-да, да, ай-да!
Ай-да, да, ай-да!
Песню солнышку поём.
Эй, эй, тяни канат смелей,
Песню солнышку поём

3. (*Refrain*)
Verse:

Эх, ты, Волга, мать-река,
Широка и глубока.
Ай-да, да, ай-да!
Ай-да, да, ай-да!
Широка и глубока.
Эй, эй, что нам всего милей,
Волга, Волга, мать-река.

2. (*Refrain*)
Verse:

My po berezhku idëm
Pesniu solnyshku roëm,
Ai-da, da, ai-da!
Ai-da, da, ai-da!
Pesniu solnyshku roëm,
Ei, ei tiani kanat smelei,
Pesniu solnyshku roëm.

3. (*Refrain*)
Verse:

Ekh, ty, Volga, mat'-reka,
Shiroka i gluboka.
Ai-da, da, ai-da!
Ai-da, da, ai-da!
Shiroka i gluboka.
Ei, ei, chto nam vsevo milei,
Volga, Volga, mat'-reka.

Part II: Popular Songs

MOSCOW NIGHTS

ПОДМОСКОВНЫЕ ВЕЧЕРА

Moderately, with feeling

Still-ness in the grove, not a rust - ling
Не слыш - ны в са - ду да - же шо - ро -
Ne slysh - ny v sa - du da - zhe sho - ro -

sound, Soft - ly shines the moon clear and bright.
хи, Всё здесь за - мер ло - до ут - ра.
khi, Vsë zdez' za - mer - lo do u - tra.

words by M. MATUSOVSKY
music by V. SOLOVYEV-SEDOY

49

2. Lazily the brook, like a silvery
      stream,
   Ripples gently in the moonlight;
   And a song afar fades as in a dream
   In the spell of this summer night.

3. Dearest, why so sad, why the
      downcast eyes,
   And your lovely head bent so low?
   Oh, it's hard to speak, and yet not
      to speak
   Of the longing my heart does know.

4. Promise me, my love, as the dawn
      appears
   And the darkness turns into light,
   That you'll cherish, dear, through
      the passing years,
   This most beautiful Moscow night.

2. Речка движется и не движется,
   Вся из лунного серебра.
   Песня слышится и не слышится
   В эти тихие вечера.

3. Что ж ты, милая, смотришь
      искоса,
   Низко голову наклоня.
   Трудно высказать и не
      высказать
   Всё, что на сердце у меня.

4. А рассвет уже всё заметнее.
   Так, пожалуйста, будь добра,
   Не забудь и ты эти летние
   Подмосковные вечера.

2. *Rechka dvizhetsia i ne dvizhetsia,*
   Vsia iz lunnovo serebra.
   Pesnia slyshitsia i ne slyshitsia
   V eti tikhie vechera.

3. *Chto zh ty, milaia, smotrish' iskosa,*
   Nizko golovu naklonia.
   Trudno vyskazat' i ne vyskazat'
   Vsë, chto na serdtse u menia.

4. *A rassvet uzhe vsë zametnee.*
   Tak, pozhaluista, bud' dobra,
   Ne zabud' i ty eti letnie
   Podmoskovnye vechera.

LONELY ACCORDION

ОДИНОКАЯ ГАРМОНЬ

words by M. ISAKOVSKY
music by B. MOKROUSOV

Waltz tempo

Once more / Cно - ва / Sno - va

night drops its cur - tain of still - ness,
за - мер - ло всё до рас - све - та,
za - mer - lo vsë do ras - sve - ta,

Not a door scrapes, no friend - ly light rays ____ Can be
дверь не скрип - нет, не вспых - нет о - гонь, ____ толь - ко
dver' ne skrip - net, ne vspykh - net o - gon', ____ tol' - ko

seen, but some - where in the dis - tance ____ Some - one's lone - ly ac -
слыш - но на у - ли - це где - то ____ о - ди - но - ка - я
slysh - no na u - li - tse gde - to ____ o - di - no - ka - ia

cor - di - on plays._____ Through the night, some-where off in the
бро - дит гар - монь._____ Толь - ко слыш - но на у - ли - це
bro - dit gar - mon'._____ Tol' - ko slysh - no na u - li - tse

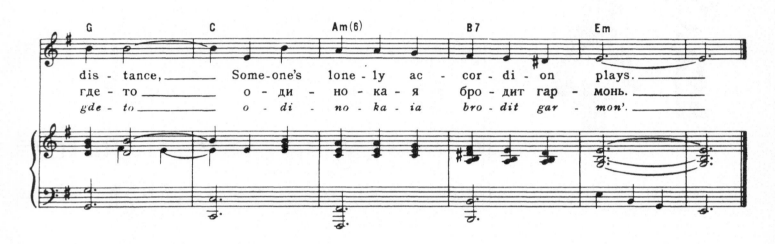

dis - tance,_____ Some-one's lone - ly ac - cor - di - on plays._____
где - то_____ о - ди - но - ка - я бро - дит гар - монь._____
gde - to_____ o - di - no - ka - ia bro - dit gar - mon'._____

2. Now it strays through the gate to the meadow,
Now it comes wandering back again,
As if seeking someone in the darkness,
Seeking, searching, but always in vain.

3. Apple blossoms are shedding their fragrance,
As the cool night air brings on the mist.
Speak and tell us, young lad, whom you're seeking,
Who is she, young accordionist?

4. It may be that your love is not far off,
Knowing nothing about your heartache;
But then, why wander lonely the whole night,
Keeping all the young maidens awake?

2. То пойдёт на поля, за ворота,
То обратно вернётся опять,
Словно ищет в потёмках кого-то
И не может никак отыскать.

3. Веет с поля ночная прохлада,
С яблонь цвет облетает густой . . .
Ты признайся, кого тебе надо,
Ты скажи, гармонист молодой.

4. Может, радость твоя недалёко,
Да не знает, её ли ты ждёшь . . .
Что ж ты бродишь всю ночь одиноко,
Что ж ты девушкам спать не даёшь!

2. *To poidët na polia, za vorota,*
To obratno vernëtsia opiat',
Slovno ishchet v potëmkakh kovo-to
I ne mozhet nikak otyskat'.

3. *Veet s polia nochnaia prokhlada,*
S iablon' tsvet obletaet gustoi . . .
Ty priznaisia, kovo tebe nado,
Ty skazhi, garmonist molodoi.

4. *Mozhet, radost' tvoia nedalëko,*
Da ne znaet, eë li ty zhdësh' . . .
Chto zh ty brodish' vsiu noch' odinoko,
Chto zh ty devushkam spat' ne daësh'!

KATIUSHA

КАТЮША

words by M. ISAKOVSKY
music by M. BLANTER

Ap-ple trees and pear trees were a-
Рас-цве-та-ли яб-ло-ни и
Ras-tsve-ta-li iab-lo-ni i

flow-er, Riv-er mist was ris-ing all a-round.
гру-ши, По-плы-ли ту-ма-ны над ре-кой.
gru-shi, Po-ply-li tu-ma-ny nad re-koi.

Young Ka-tiu-sha went stroll-ing by the hour__ On the steep banks, o'er the rock-y ground.
Вы-хо-ди-ла на бе-рег Ка-тю-ша, На вы-со-кий бе-рег, на кру-той.
Vy-kho-di-la na be-reg Ka-tiu-sha, Na vy-so-kii be-reg, na kru-toi.

2. By the river's bank she sang a love song
Of her hero in a distant land.
Of the one she'd dearly loved for so long,
Holding tight his letters in her hand.

2. Выходила, песню заводила
Про степного сизого орла,
Про того, которого любила,
Про того, чьи письма берегла.

2. *Vykhodila, pesniu zavodila*
Pro stepnovo sizovo orla,
Pro tovo, kotorovo liubila,
Pro tovo, ch'i pis'ma beregla.

3. Oh, my song, song of a maiden's true love,
   To my dear one travel with the sun.
   To the one with whom Katiusha knew love,
   Bring my greetings to him, one by one.

4. Let him know that I am true and faithful,
   Let him hear the love song that I send.
   Tell him as he defends our home, that grateful,
   True Katiusha our love will defend.

5. (*Repeat first verse*)

3. Ой ты, песня, песенка девичья,
   Ты лети за ясным солнцем вслед,
   И бойцу на дальнем пограничье
   От Катюши передай привет.

4. Пусть он вспомнит девушку простую,
   Пусть услышит, как она поёт,
   Пусть он землю бережёт родную,
   А любовь Катюша сбережёт.

5. (*Повторить первый куплет*)

3. *Oi ty, pesnia, pesenka devichia,*
   Ty leti za iasnym solntsem vsled,
   I boitsu na dal'nem pogranich'e
   Ot Katiushi peredai privet.

4. *Pust' on vspomnit devushku prostuiu,*
   Pust' uslyshit, kak ona poët,
   Pust' on zemliu berezhët rodnuiu,
   A liubov' Katiusha sberezhët.

5. (*Repeat first verse*)

Moderately

Wait for me and I'll come back. Wait! Have faith and
Жди ме-ня и я вер-нусь, Толь-ко о-чень
Zhdi me-nia i ia ver-nus', Tol'-ko o-chen'

wait. Wait when gloom-y au-tumn rains
жди. Жди, ког-да на-во-дят грусть
zhdi. Zhdi, kog-da na-vo-diat grust'

WAIT FOR ME

ЖДИ МЕНЯ

words by K. SIMONOV
music by M. BLANTER

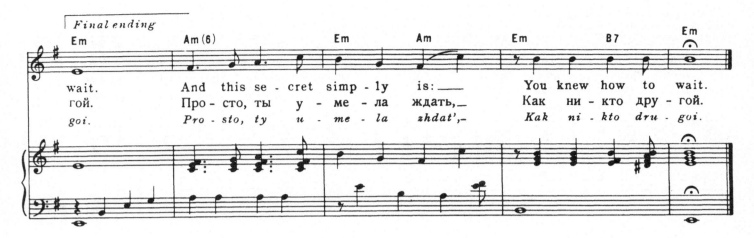

wait. And this se-cret simp-ly is:___ You knew how to wait.
гой. Про-сто, ты у-ме-ла ждать,___ Как ни-кто дру-гой.
goi. Pro-sto, ty u-me-la zhdat',— Kak ni-kto dru-goi.

2. Wait for me and I'll return;
   Do not grieve for me.
   Listen not to those who sigh
   And weep mournfully.
   Let my son, my mother think
   I lie deep in mire;
   Let all those who hope have lost,
   Sitting 'round the fire,
   Sadly drink of bitter wine,
   And for my soul pray.
   But, dear, hasten not to drink—
   I'll be back one day.

2. Жди меня, и я вернусь,
   Не желай добра
   Всем, кто знает наизусть,
   Что забыть пора.
   Пусть поверят сын и мать
   В то, что нет меня.
   Пусть друзья устанут ждать,
   Сядут у огня,
   Выпьют горькое вино
   На помин души . . .
   Жди — и с ними заодно
   Выпить не спеши.

2. Zhdi menia, i ia vernus',
   Ne zhelai dobra
   Vsem, kto znaet naizust',
   Chto zabyt' pora.
   Pust' poveriat syn i mat'
   V to, chto net menia.
   Pust' druz'ia ustanut zhdat',
   Siadut u ognia,
   Vyp'iut gor'koe vino
   Na pomin dushi . . .
   Zhdi—i s nimi zaodno
   Vypit' ne speshi.

3. Wait for me, I'm coming back;
   Death will not win me.
   Those who would not wait will cry:
   Fortunate is he!
   They will never understand
   How through battle's hell,
   By your steadfast waiting, dear,
   My life you held well.
   How this happened just we two
   Know the secret great.
   And the secret simply is:
   You knew how to wait.

3. Жди меня, и я вернусь
   Всем смертям назло.
   Кто не ждал меня, тот пусть
   Скажет: «Повезло».
   Не понять не ждавшим, им,
   Как среди огня
   Ожиданием своим
   Ты спасла меня.
   Как я выжил — будем знать
   Только мы с тобой.
   Просто, ты умела ждать,
   Как никто другой.

3. Zhdi menia, i ia vernus',
   Vsem smertiam nazlo.
   Kto ne zhdal menia, tot pust'
   Skazhet: "Povezlo".
   Ne poniat' ne zhdavshim, im,
   Kak sredi ognia
   Ozhidaniem svoim
   Ty spasla menia.
   Kak ia vyzhil—budem znat'
   Tol'ko my s toboi.
   Prosto, ty umela zhdat',
   Kak nikto drugoi.

SILENTLY

ТИШИНА

words by V. ORLOV
music by E. KOLMANOVSKY

Moderately and freely

At the win-dow beats the storm-y night,
Но-чью за ок-ном ме-тель, ме-тель,
No-ch'iu za ok-nom me-tel', me-tel',

White and ev-er shift-ing snow.
Бе-лый бес-по-кой-ный снег.
Be-lyi bes-po-koi-nyi sneg.

You are man-y worlds a-way, you've quite
Ты жи-вёшь за три-де-вять зе-мель,
Ty zhi-vёsh' za tri-de-viat' ze-mel',

Cut me out of ev-'ry thought I
Ты не вспо-ми-на-ешь о-бо
Ty ne vspo-mi-na-esh' o-bo

know.
мне.
mne.

I know that I'll nev-er hear from you.
Зна-ю я, ни строч-ки не при-дёт,
Zna-iu ia ni stroch-ki ne pri-dёt,

You don't need that mem - o - ry.
Па - мять боль - ше не нуж - на.
Pa - miat' bol' - she ne nuzh - na.

Through the cit - y I will wan - der,
По боль - шо - му го - ро - ду бре -
Po bol' - sho - mu go - ro - du bre -

4th time play without vocal till ⊕, then sing final 4 lines

blue —
дёт
dёt

Si - lent - ly.
Ти - ши - на.
Ti - shi - na.

Si - lent - ly. _____
Ти - ши - на. _____
Ti - shi - na. _____

2. It's been long since you were
    standing near,
   There is no more path to you.
   Happiness comes only once, my
    dear;
   Only I did not know what to do.
   Nighttime brings me pain instead
    of rest;
   Conscience hurts me bitterly.
   I look out my window hoping for
    the best—
   Silently.

2. Ты меня не ждёшь давным-
    давно,
   Нет к тебе путей-дорог.
   Счастье у людей всего одно,
   Только я его не уберёг.
   Ночью мне покоя не даёт
   Горькая моя вина.
   Ночью за окном звенит, поёт
   Тишина . . .

2. *Ty menia ne zhdёsh' davnym-
    davno,*
   Net k tebe putei-dorog.
   Schast'e u liudei vsevo odno,
   Tol'ko ia evo ne uberёg.
   Noch'iu mne pokoia ne daёt
   Gor'kaia moia vina.
   Noch'iu za oknom zvenit, poёt
   Tishina . . .

3. If I could but find out where you
    live,
   Find you in some foreign land.
   Only just to ask you, "Please
    forgive,"
   And to take hold of your beloved
    hand.
   Oh, to tell you how through all the
    nights
   Sleep has never come to me.
   Now I wait here in my room without
    the lights—
   Silently.

4. Then you would know how through
    all the nights
   Sleep has never come to me.
   Now I wait here in my room without
    the lights—
   Silently.

3. Только б мне тебя найти, найти,
   Отыскать в любом краю,
   Только бы сказать тебе
    «прости»,
   Руку взять любимую твою,
   Рассказать, как ночи напролёт,
   Летом и зимой — без сна,
   Здесь тебя со мною вместе ждёт
   Тишина . . .

4. Знала б ты, как ночи напролёт,
   Летом и зимой — без сна
   Здесь тебя со мною вместе ждёт
   Тишина . . .

3. *Tol'ko b mne tebia naiti, naiti,*
   Otyskat' v liubom kraiu,
   Tol'ko by skazat' tebe "prosti",
   Ruku vziat' liubimuiu tvoiu,
   Rasskazat', kak nochi naprolët,
   Letom i zimoi—bez sna,
   Zdes' tebia so mnoiu vmeste zhdët
   Tishina . . .

4. *Znala b ty, kak nochi naprolët,*
   Letom i zimoi—bez sna,
   Zdes' tebia so mnoiu vmeste zhdët
   Tishina . . .

DARK IS THE NIGHT

ТЕМНАЯ НОЧЬ

words by V. AGATOV
music by N. BOGOSLAVSKY

2. How I believe in your love, dearest
   sweetheart of mine.
   And this faith, like a charm, keeps
   me safe through the fires of battle.
   Peaceful and calm do I feel, though
   the fighting is fierce,
   For I know you will meet me with
   love, dear, no matter what
   happens.
   I fear not death,—many times we
   have met in the field;
   And even now, as he circles and
   whirls about me,
   I know that you at the cradle are
   waiting, awake.
   And because, dear, I know you
   are there, I'll come back to you
   safely.

2. Верю в тебя, в дорогую подругу
   мою
   Эта вера от пули меня тёмной
   ночью хранила.
   Радостно мне, я спокоен в
   смертельном бою,
   Знаю, встретишь с любовью
   меня, что б со мной ни
   случилось.
   Смерть не страшна, с ней не раз
   мы встречались в степи,
   Вот и теперь надо мною она
   кружится . . .
   Ты меня ждёшь и у детской
   кроватки не спишь,
   И поэтому, знаю, со мной
   ничего не случится!

2. *Veriu v tebia, v doroguiu podrugu
   moiu*
   *Eta vera ot puli menia tëmnoi
   noch'iu khranila.*
   *Radostno mne, ia spokoen v
   smertel'nom boiu,*
   *Znaiu, vstretish' s liubov'iu menia,
   chto b so mnoi ni sluchilos'.*
   *Smert' ne strashna, s nei ne raz
   my vstrechalis' v stepi,*
   *Vot i teper' nado mnoiu ona
   kruzhitsia . . .*
   *Ty menia zhdësh' i u detskoi
   krovatki ne spish',*
   *I poetomu, znaiu, so mnoi
   nichevo ne sluchitsia!*

STRAINS OF GUITAR (ON THE RIVER)

ЗВЕНИТ ГИТАРА НАД РЕКОЮ

words by A. OSHANIN
music by A. NOVIKOV

2. Within us thoughts are speeding
    onward,
Soon distant shores come into sight.
Your spreading palm trees rise
    before us,
My curly birch trees, snows so
    white.
Though different be our way of
    living,
And different, too, our lands of
    birth,
The dreams we have all blend
    together,
Though between us lies half the
    earth.
    (Chorus)

3. Strains of guitar upon the river,
Soft flows the river in the night.
And sitting side by side together,
A dark-skinned hand in one so
    white.
How swift the hour comes for our
    parting;
No more to meet—or who knows
    when?
But heart with heart must come
    together,
And some day, surely, meet again.
    (Chorus)

2. И вот как будто мчимся
        вдаль мы,
Встают иные берега —
Твои раскидистые пальмы,
Мои берёзы и снега.
И всё у нас с тобой иное,
И мы по-разному росли,

Но мы живём мечтой одною,
Хоть между нами полземли.
    (Chorus)

3. Звенит гитара над рекою,
И не спеша бежит река.
И рядом с белою рукою
Темнеет смуглая рука.
Пускай придёт пора проститься,
Друг друга долго не видать,
Но сердце с сердцем, словно
        птицы,
Конечно, встретятся опять.
    (Chorus)

2. *I vot kak budto mchimsia vdal' my,*
Vstaiut inye berega—
Tvoi raskidistye palmy,
Moi berëzy i snega.
I vsë u nas s toboi inoe,
I my po raznomu rosli,
No my zhivëm mechtoi odnoiu,
Khot' mezhdu nami polzemli.
    (Chorus)

3. *Zvenit gitara nad rekoiu,*
I ne spesha bezhit reka.
I riadom s beloiu rukoiu
Temneet smuglaia ruka.
Puskai pridët pora prostit'sia,
Drug druga dolgo ne vidat',
No serdtse s serdtsem, slovno
        ptitsy,
Konechno, vstretiatsia opiat'.
    (Chorus)

THE LIGHT

ОГОНЕК

words by M. ISAKOVSKY
composer unknown

Moderately

A young sol-dier and maid are sad,
На по-зи-ци-и де-вуш-ка
Na po-zi-tsi-i de-vush-ka

Soon he'll leave for the war.
Про-во-жа-ла бой-ца,
Pro-vo-zha-la boi-tsa,

Dark the night when they
Тём-ной ночь-ю про-
Tëm-noi noch'-iu pro-

said good-bye
сти-ла-ся
sti-la-sia

On the steps at her door.
На сту-пень-ках кры-льца.
Na stu-pen'-kakh kry-l'tsa.

As he walked a-way
И по-ка за ту-
I po-ka za tu-

he could see,
ма-на-ми
ma-na-mi

Through the dark mist-y night,
Ви-деть мог па-ре-нёк,
Vi-det' mog pa-re-nëk,

Like a bea-con from
На о-кош-ке на
Na o-kosh-ke na

her win-dow   Shin-ing bright-ly, a   light.   light.
де - ви-чьем   Всё го- рел о-го-нёк.   нёк
de - vi-ch'em   Vsë go-rel o-go-nëk.   nëk.

2. At the front he met all his friends,
Fellow soldiers were they.
All about him were his comrades,
Side by side night and day.
But the dear, old familiar face
Ever was in his sight:
"Where, oh, where are you, my dear
    one?
Where is my little light?"

3. Then from his sweetheart faraway
Did a letter appear:
"My love for you will never die,
That is my vow, my dear.
All our hope, all the dreams we've
    had
Are with me clear and bright,
And till you're back they'll shine
    for me
In my bright golden light."

4. Filled with happiness, overjoyed,
The brave lad's heart did soar
At the wonderful words of love
His sweetheart's letter bore.
And with his hated enemy
With new vigor does fight,
For his own native Soviet Land,
For his dear little light.

2. Парня встретила славная
Фронтовая семья.
Всюду были товарищи,
Всюду были друзья,
Но знакомую улицу
Позабыть он не мог:
«Где ж ты, девушка милая,
Где ж ты, мой огонёк?»

3. И подруга далёкая
Парню весточку шлёт,
Что любовь её девичья
Никогда не умрёт.
Всё, что было загадано,
В свой исполнится срок,
Не погаснет без времени
Золотой огонёк.

4. И просторно и радостно
На душе у бойца
От такого хорошего,
От её письмеца.
И врага ненавистного
Крепче бьёт паренёк
За советскую Родину,
За родной огонёк.

2. *Parnia vstretila slavnaia*
Frontovaia sem'ia.
Vsiudu byli tovarishchi,
Vsiudu byli druz'ia,
No znakomuiu ulitsu
Pozabyt' on ne mog:
"Gde zh ty, devushka milaia,
Gde zh ty, moi ogonëk?"

3. *I podruga dalëkaia*
Parniu vestochku shlët,
Chto liubov' eë devich'ia
Nikogda ne umrët.
Vsë, chto bylo zagadano,
V svoi ispolnitsia srok,
Ne pogasnet bez vremeni
Zolotoi ogonëk.

4. *I prostorno i radostno*
Na dushe u boitsa
Ot takovo khoroshevo,
Ot eë pis'metsa.
I vraga nenavistnovo
Krepche b'ët parenëk
Za sovetskuiu Rodinu,
Za rodnoi ogonëk.

WAIT FOR YOUR SOLDIER

ЖДИ СОЛДАТА

words by S. OSTROV
music by B. MOKROUSOV

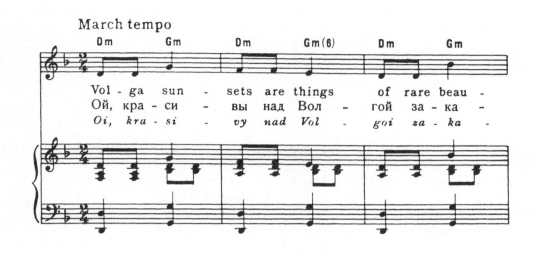

Volga sunsets are things of rare beauty, But your soldier must now do his duty. Press my hand, dear, See me off, dear, See me off, dear, See me off, dear.

Ой, красивы над Волгой закаты... Ты меня провожала в солдаты. Руку жала, Провожала, Провожала, Провожала.

Oi, krasivy nad Volgoi zakaty... Ty menia provozhala v soldaty. Ruku zhala, Provozhala, Provozhala, Provozhala.

2. With our cherished old pine tree
     above you
   As we part, you must know how I
     love you.
   Forget never,
   Yours forever.

3. As the train started off on its long
     ride,
   You were waving your hand from
     the hillside.
   Far-off places,
   Endless spaces.

4. Now a soldier's sweetheart, dear,
     believe me,
   Must be brave—and I know you'll
     not grieve me.
   You must wait, dear,
   It is fate, dear.

5. Oh, the days to a soldier seems
     endless,
   But I know you will not leave me
     friendless.
   How I want you,
   How I need you.

6. Oh, how long can I go on without
     her?
   I have told all my buddies about
     her.
   Infantrymen,
   Brave and free men.

7. Once more to the front I must go,
     dear;
   You'll be waiting at home—that I
     know, dear.
   Waiting for your
   Soldier warrior.

2. Под густой, под заветной
     сосною
   Ты до звёзд простояла со мною.
   Помнить буду,
   Не забуду.

3. Застучали по рельсам колёса,
   Ты рукой мне махнула с откоса.
   Ширь степная,
   Даль без края.

4. Ты подружкой солдатской
     зовёшься,
   Значит, верю — меня ты
     дождёшься.
   Ждать ты станешь,
   Не обманешь.

5. У солдата суровая служба,
   Так нужна ему девичья дружба!
   Чем нежнее,
   Тем нужнее.

6. О подружке моей чернобровой
   Знают все в нашей роте
     стрелковой.
   Наша рота,
   Эх, пехота.

7. Я родную страну охраняю,
   Ты дождёшься солдата, я знаю!
   Помни свято —
   Жди солдата.

2. *Pod gustoi, pod zavetnoi sosnoiu*
   Ty do zvëzd prostoiala so mnoiu.
   Pomnit' budu,
   Ne zabudu.

3. *Zastuchali po rel'sam kolësa,*
   Ty rukoi mne makhnula s otkosa.
   Shir' stepnaia,
   Dal' bez kraia.

4. *Ty podruzhkoi soldatskoi*
     zovësh'sia,
   Znachit, veriu—menia ty
     dozhdësh'sia.
   Zhdat' ty stanesh',
   Ne obmanesh'.

5. *U soldata surovaia sluzhba,*
   Tak nuzhna emu devich'ia druzhba!
   Chem nezhnee,
   Tem nuzhnee.

6. *O podruzhke moei chernobrovoi*
   Znaiut vse v nashei rote strelkovoi.
   Nasha rota,
   Ekh, pekhota.

7. *Ia rodnuiu stranu okhraniaiu,*
   Ty dozhdësh'sia soldata, ia znaiu!
   Pomni sviato—
   Zhdi soldata.

MEADOWLAND

ПОЛЮШКО-ПОЛЕ

words by V. GUSEV
music by L. KNIPPER

March tempo

O — pen fields, bound — less plains,
По — люш-ко-по — ле (ды),
Po — liush-ko — po — le (dy),

O-pen fields and end-less prai-rie; There go a-cross the fields the
По-люш-ко, ши-ро-ко по-ле, Е — дут(ы) по по-лю ге-
Po-liush-ko, shi-ro-ko po-le. E — dut (y) po po-liu ge-

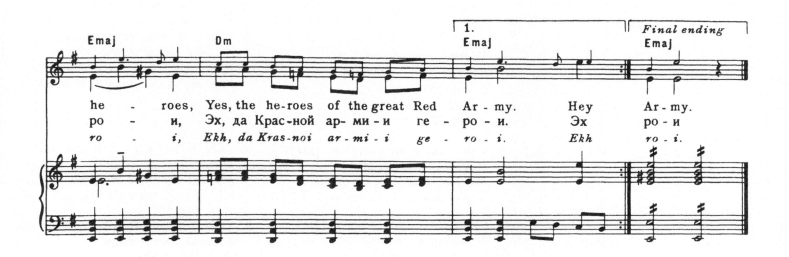

he — roes, Yes, the he-roes of the great Red Ar — my. Hey Ar — my.
ро — и, Эх, да Крас-ной ар-ми-и ге — ро-и. Эх ро — и
ro — i, Ekh, da Kras-noi ar-mi-i ge — ro-i. Ekh ro — i.

Alternate left hand

etc.

2. Young girls are crying,
   All the girls today are mournful.
   Sweethearts rode out with the army,
   Yes, they'll be long gone with the army.

3. Girls, raise your eyes up;
   Follow with your eyes our journey,
   See how the distant road goes winding,
   Yes, the joyous open highway.

4. Girls, raise your eyes up;
   Wipe away the tears of sorrow.
   Let's sing together even louder,
   Yes, our song of battle even louder.

5. (*Repeat first verse*)
   Note: These verses are abridged adaptations of the Russian lyrics.

---

2. (Эх-) Девушки плачут (ы),
   Девушкам сегодня грустно,
   Милый (ды) надолго уехал,
   Эх, да милый в армию уехал.

3. (Эх-) Девушки, гляньте (ды),
   Гляньте на дорогу нашу,
   Вьётся (ды) дальняя дорога,
   Эх, да развесёлая дорога.

4. (Эх-) Едем мы, едем (ды),
   Едем, — а кругом колхозы,
   Наши (ды), девушки, колхозы,
   Эх, да молодые наши сёла.

5. (Эх-) Только мы видим (ды),
   Видим мы седую тучу,
   Вражья (ды) злоба из-за леса,
   Эх, да вражья злоба, словно туча.

6. (Эх-) Девушки, гляньте (ды),
   Мы врага принять готовы,
   Наши (ды) кони быстроноги,
   Эх, да наши танки быстроходны.

7. (Эх-) В небе за тучей (ды)
   Грозные следят пилоты,
   Быстро (ды) плавают подлодки,
   Эх, да зорко смотрит Ворошилов.

8. (Эх-) Пусть же в колхозе (ды)
   Дружная кипит работа,
   Мы (ы) дозорные сегодня,
   Эх, да мы сегодня часовые.

9. (Эх-) Девушки, гляньте (ды),
   Девушки, утрите слёзы.
   Пусть (ы) сильнее грянет песня,
   Эх, да наша песня боевая.

10. (Эх-) Полюшко-поле (ды),
    Полюшко, зелёно поле.
    Едут (ы) по полю герои,
    Эх, да Красной армии герои.

---

2. (*Ekh-*) *Devushki plachut* (*y*),
   Devushkam sevodnia grustno,
   Milyi (*dy*) *nadolgo uekhal,*
   Ekh, da milyi v armiiu uekhal.

3. (*Ekh-*) *Devushki, glian'te* (*dy*),
   Glian'te na dorogu nashu,
   V'ëtsia (*dy*) *dal'niaia doroga,*
   Ekh, da razvesëlaia doroga.

4. (*Ekh-*) *Edem my, edem* (*dy*),
   Edem,—a krugom kolkhozy,
   Nashi (*dy*), *devushki, kolkhozy,*
   Ekh, da molodye nashi sëla.

5. (*Ekh-*) *Tol'ko my vidim* (*dy*),
   Vidim my seduiu tuchu,
   Vrazh'ia (*dy*) *zloba iz-za lesa,*
   Ekh, da vrazh'ia zloba, slovno tucha.

6. (*Ekh-*) *Devushki, glian'te* (*dy*),
   My vraga priniat' gotovy,
   Nashi (*dy*) *koni bystronogi,*
   Ekh, da nashi tanki bystrokhodny.

7. (*Ekh-*) *V nebe za tuchei* (*dy*)
   Groznye slediat piloty,
   Bystro (*dy*) *plavaiut podlodki,*
   Ekh, da zorko smotrit Voroshilov.

8. (*Ekh-*) *Pust' zhe v kolkhoze* (*dy*)
   Druzhnaia kipit rabota,
   My (*y*) *dozornye sevodnia,*
   Ekh, da my sevodnia chasovye.

9. (*Ekh-*) *Devushki, glian'te* (*dy*)
   Devushki, utrite slëzy.
   Pust' (*y*) *sil'nee grianet pesnia,*
   Ekh, da nasha pesnia boevaia.

10. (*Ekh-*) *Poliushko-pole* (*dy*),
    Poliushko, zelëno pole.
    Edut (*y*) *po poliu geroi,*
    Ekh, da Krasnoi armii geroi.

REGIMENTAL POLKA

ГВАРДЕЙСКАЯ ПОЛЬКА

words by V. GURYAN
music by B. TERENTIEV

Not fast—with spirit

When the sol-diers stopped
На сол - дат-ском при -
Na sol - dat-skom pri -

hik - ing, With mu-sic more their lik - ing, Soon a
ва - ле, Ба - я-ны за - и - гра-ли, По-да -
va - le, Ba - ia-ny za - i - gra-li, Po-da -

pol - ka was re - quest-ed, And fan-cy steps were test-ed. Well, the
ла ко-ман-ду «Поль-ка»: Тан-цуй-те, да и толь-ко! По-ле -
la ko-man-du "Pol'-ka": Tan-tsui-te, da i tol'-ko! Po-le -

coat tails were sail - ing, And heav-y boots were flail-ing, As the
те - ли ши - не - ли, Под-ков-ки за-зве-не-ли, В у-да -
te - li shi - ne - li, Pod-kov-ki za-zve-ne-li, V u-da -

CHORUS

2. Seeing soldiers dance madly,
   A young lad murmured sadly,
   "Boys, I don't mind all this
      prancing,
   But with girls we'd have *real*
      dancing."
   The lance corporal, laughing,
   Said, "I know just the right thing—
   Wear this kerchief and this shawl
      now,
   And you could fool us all now!"
      Never mind how little
      Time we have for our victuals.
      Never mind, my buddy
      That our boots are hot and
   muddy.
   (*Chorus*)

2. Замечтался некстати
   Молоденький солдатик:
   «Кабы имелись дамы,
   «Сплясали бы тогда мы» . . .
   А ефрейтор хохочет:
   «Повязывай платочек,
   С кавалером чин по чину
   Станцуешь за дивчину!»
   Не беда, что мало
   Короткого привала!
   Не беда, солдаты,
   Что сапоги тяжеловаты!
   (*Chorus*)

2. *Zamechtalsia nekstati*
   Moloden'kii soldatik:
   "Kaby imelis' damy,
   Spliasali by togda my" . . .
   A efreitor khokhochet:
   "Poviazyvai platochek,
   S kavalerom chin po chinu
   Stantsuesh' za divchinu!"
   Ne beda, chto malo
   Korotkovo privala!
   Ne beda, soldaty,
   Chto sapogi tiazhelovaty!
   (*Chorus*)

3. Then a sturdy young sergeant
   Was grabbed by two lieutenants,
   And they said that they just never
   Had seen one quite so clever.
   Now, three Moscow musicians,
   They play with such precision
   That your feet, they fairly yank
     you—
   Accordionists, thank you!
     Never mind that at hand
     No chandeliers and brass band.
     On the road we've all room
     To dance like we're in the grand
     ballroom.
     (*Chorus*)

3. Подхватили сержанта
   Два бравых лейтенанта —
   Наилучшего партнёра
   Нашли они без спора . . .
   Три московских баяна
   Наяривают рьяно,
   Хорошо плясать с присвистом,
   Спасибо баянистам!
   Не беда, что нету
   Ни люстры, ни паркету,
   На любом привале
   Танцуем как в Колонном зале!
     (*Chorus*)

3. *Podkhvatili serzhanta*
   Dva bravykh leitenanta—
   Nailuchshevo partnёra
   Nashli oni bez spora . . .
   Tri moskovskikh baiana
   Naiarivaiut r'iano,
   Khorosho pliasat' s prisvistom,
   Spasibo baianistam!
   Ne beda, chto nεtu
   Ni liustry, ni parketu,
   Na liubom privale
   Tantsuem kak v Kolonnom zale!
     (*Chorus*)

Moderately

How man-y sweet and ten-der maid-ens,
Как мно-го де-ву-шек хо-ро-ших,
Kak mno-go de-vu-shek kho-ro-shikh,

How man-y sweet and love-ly names.
Как мно-го лас-ко-вых и-мён,
Kak mno-go las-ko-vykh i-mёn,

MY HEART

КАК МНОГО ДЕВУШЕК ХОРОШИХ (СЕРДЦЕ)

words by V. LEBEDEV-KUMACH
music by I. DUNAYEVSKY

FAR AWAY, FAR AWAY

ДАЛЕКО, ДАЛЕКО

words by A. CHURKIN
music by G. NOSOV

With Movement, with Agitation

Far a-way, far a - way, _____ Where the gray fogs are
Да-ле-ко, да-ле-ко, _____ Где ко-чу-ют ту-
Da-le-ko, da-le-ko, _____ Gde ko-chu-iut tu-

drift - ing, _____ Where the calm sum-mer breez - es The
ма - ны, _____ Где от лёг-ко-го вет - ра Ко-
ma - ny, _____ Gde ot lëg-ko-vo vet - ra Ko-

gold - en rye sway. _____ I see you all a - lone _____
лы - шет-ся рожь, _____ Ты в ро-ди-мом кра - ю _____
ly - shet-sia rozh', _____ Ty v ro-di-mom kra - iu _____

_Stand-ing sad-ly at your door, _____ Ev - er think-ing of me, _____ dear, Live
У степ-но-го кур-га - на, _____ О-бо мне вспо-ми - на - я, Как
_U step-no-vo kur-ga - na, _____ O-bo mne vspo-mi - na - ia, Kak

let - ter _____ From your friend far a - way. _____
лан - ной. _____ Ты всё вес - точ - ки ждёшь. _____
lan - noi _____ *Ty vsë ves - toch - ki zhdesh'.* _____

Final ending   *rit.*

dar - ling, _____ that I think night and day. _____
серд - це, _____ я за - быть не мо - гу. _____
serd - tse, _____ *ia za - byt' ne mo - gu.* _____

2. Endless skies spread above,
  Vast and boundless my home land.
  Rivers swiftly rush on,
  Mingle with the sea sand.
  Oh, dear land of my birth,
  Your great strength overpowers.
  My beloved home, my Russia—
  This land is all ours.
    And of you, my dear bright eyes,
    Oh, my sunshine, my fair one.
    On this faraway border,
    I keep dreaming of you.

3. Far away, far away,
  Where gray forests are standing,
  Your hopes, dreams and your peace,
    dear,
  I'll guard without end.
  And the beast on the prowl,
  If he enters our home land,
  To his end must be sent—
  That is our command.
    In these times of great peril,
    At the front in the trenches,
    'Tis of you, my own darling
    That I think night and day.

2. Небосвод над тобой
  Опрокинулся синий,
  Плещут быстрые реки,
  Вздыхают моря.
  Широко протянулась
  Большая Россия —
  Дорогая отчизна
  Твоя и моя.
    О тебе, светлоокой,
    Моей зорьке красивой
    На далёкой границе
    Вновь задумался я.

3. Далеко, далеко,
  За лесами седыми,
  Я твой сон и покой
  Всякий час берегу,
  Чтоб звериной тропой,
  В край навеки родимый,
  Не пройти никогда
  Никакому врагу.
    В нашей жизни тревожной
    Пограничной заставы
    О тебе, моё сердце,
    Я забыть не могу.

2. *Nebosvod nad toboi*
  Oprokinulsia sinii,
  Pleshchut bystrye reki,
  Vzdykhaiut moria.
  Shiroko protianulas'
  Bol'shaia Rossiia—
  Dorogaia otchizna
  Tvoia i moia.
    O tebe, svetlookoi,
    Moei zor'ke krasivoi
    Na dalëkoi granitse
    Vnov' zadumalsia ia.

3. *Daleko, daleko,*
  Za lesami sedymi,
  Ia tvoi son i pokoi
  Vsiakii chas beregu,
  Chtob zverinoi tropoi,
  V krai, naveki rodimyi,
  Ne proiti nikogda
  Nikakomu vragu.
    V nashei zhizni trevozhnoi
    Pogranichnoi zastavy
    O tebe, moë serdtse,
    Ia zabyt' ne mogu.

SHOULD THE VOLGA'S BANKS BE FLOODED

ЕСЛИ ВОЛГА РАЗОЛЬЕТСЯ

words by V. LEBEDEV-KUMACH
music by I. DUNAYEVSKY

Moderately, with expression

How much sor - row, how much tor - ment Can one's
Мно - го го - ря и стра - дань - я Серд - це
Mno - go go - ria i stra - dan' - ia Serd - tse

heart in love en - dure? When he tells you, "See you
тер - пит не - взна - чай. Ми - лый ска - жет: «До сви -
ter - pit ne - vzna - chai. Mil - yi ska - zhet: "Do svi -

la - ter," It's "Fare-well," your heart is sure. You can't guess_____ but on - ly
дани - я,» Серд - це слы - шит «... И про - щай.» На - пе - рёд_____ не у - га -
dani - ia," Serd - tse sly - shit"... I pro - shchai." Na - pe - rëd_____ ne u - ga -

pon - der What your des - ti - ny will be: Love and
да - ешь, Где судь - бу_____ сво - ю най - дёшь, Коль по -
da - esh', Gde sud' - bu_____ svo - iu nai - dësh', Kol' po -

With - out love how hard the liv - ing, Hard-er still when you're in love.
Без люб- ви на све - те труд- но, А лю- бить е-щё труд- ней.
Bez liu-bvi na sve-te trud-no, A liu-bit' e-shchë trud-nei.

2. I am young and have a problem:
What to do, oh, what to do?
And I'm truly in great trouble—
Cannot tell him, "I love you."
He'll be vain if I love too well;
If not too well he may leave.
If he's too gay I'll be jealous,
If he's solemn I may grieve.
   (*Chorus*)

2. Я девчонка молодая,
Что мне делать, как мне быть?
Оттого я и страдаю,
Что не знаю, как любить:
Крепко любишь — избалуешь,
Мало любишь — отпугнёшь,
Беспокойный — ты ревнуешь,
А спокойный — нехорош.
   (*Chorus*)

2. *Ia devchonka molodaia,*
Chto mne delat', kak mne byt'?
Ottovo ia i stradaiu,
Chto ne znaiu, kak liubit':
Krepko liubish'—izbaluesh',
Malo liubish'—otpugnësh',
Bespokoinyi—ty revnuesh',
A spokoinyi—nekhorosh.
   (*Chorus*)

3. Happiness a little bird is,
Without cage or sheltering nest.
Like a match that flares and flickers;
Like a star it oft shines best.
Salt there must be with your eating;
Buy whatever you may crave.
If you love you are its slave.
Happiness ofttimes brings
   heartaches—
   (*Chorus*)

3. Счастье — птичка-невеличка,
Нет ни клетки, ни гнезда,
То погаснет, точно спичка,
То зажжётся, как звезда.
Нету кушанья без соли,
Если вышла — так купи,
Нету радости без боли,
Если любишь — так терпи.
   (*Chorus*)

3. *Schast'e—ptichka-nevelichka,*
Net ni kletki, ni gnezda,
To pogasnet, tochno spichka,
To zazhzhëtsia, kak zvezda.
Netu kushan'ia bez soli,
Esli vyshla—tak kupi,
Netu radosti bez boli,
Esli liubish'—tak terpi.
   (*Chorus*)

4. Could it be my taste is changing?
I can't think my problem through.
Hazel eyes last night I dreamed of,
Now I dream of eyes of blue.
Can one love a man that's little,
Love for him is bound to lag;
You must stoop to kiss his
   forehead—
You can keep him in your bag.
   (*Chorus*)

4. Видно, вкус мой изменился,
Что поделать мне с собой?
Карий глаз вчера приснился,
А сегодня — голубой.
Трудно в маленьких
   влюбляться,
Как их будешь обожать:
Целоваться — нагибаться,
Провожать — в карман сажать.
   (*Chorus*)

4. *Vidno vkus moi izmenilsia,*
Chto podelat' mne s soboi?
Karii glaz vchera prisnilsia,
A sevodnia—goluboi.
Trudno v malen'kikh vliubliat'sia,
Kak ikh budesh' obozhat':
Tselovat'sia—nagibat'sia,
Provozhat'—v karman sazhat'.
   (*Chorus*)

STROLLING HOME

ПРОВОЖАНЬЕ

words by M. ISAKOVSKY
music by V. ZAKHAROV

Calmly

Oh, hand me my ac - cor - di -
Ох, дай - те в ру - ки мне гар -
Okh, dai - te v ru - ki mne gar -

on, _____ Gold - en-voiced and heart - y.
монь _____ Зо - ло - ты - е план - ки!
mon' _____ Zo - lo - ty - e plan - ki!

Oh, a young man and his best girl _____ Stroll-ing from a par - ty.
Ох, па - рень дев - уш - ку до - мой _____ Про - во - жал с гу - лян - ки.
Okh, pa - ren' dev - ush - ku do - moi _____ Pro - vo - zhal s gu - lian - ki.

Hand in hand they walked a - long_ Hap - pi - ly_ to - geth - er,
Шли о - ни в ру - ке ру - ка _____ Ве - се - ло и друж - но,
Shli o - ni v ru - ke ru - ka _____ Ve - se - lo i druzh - no,

But the_ path_ was much too_ short, They could have strolled for - ev - er.
Толь - ко_ стёж - ка ко - рот - ка: Рас - ста - вать - ся нуж - но.
Tol' - ko_ stëzh - ka ko - rot - ka: Ras - sta - vat' - sia nuzh - no.

2. All too soon appeared her house
   With its windows darkened.
   Oh, you path, please wait awhile,
   To my song, please hearken.
       Hey, young fellow, take your time,
       Youth with eyes of gray.
       What a pity, what a shame,
       So soon to go away.

3. Then, hand me my accordion
   And I'll play it mellow.
   Strolling down a country path,
   A young girl and her fellow.
       Hand in hand they walked along,
       They were homeward going.
       But somehow they lost their way
       By the river flowing.

4. He forgot the well-known road,
   Oh, the playful lover.
   One road led to Katya's house,
   So he took the other.
       Oh, the river flows deep and wide,
       Only look and listen.
       Now they pause and side by side
       Kolya and Katya kissin'.

5. To return home last of all,
   Katya feels is not right.
   But her feet, her little feet,
   Will not move just for spite.
       How they want to linger on,
       See the rising moon now.
       Oh, my old accordion,
       Play just one more tune now.

2. Хата встала впереди,
   Тёмное окошко.
   Ох ты, стёжка, погоди,
   Протянись немножко!
       Ты потише провожай,
       Парень сероглазый,
       Потому что очень жаль
       Расставаться сразу.

3. Дайте ж в руки мне гармонь,
   Чтоб сыграть страданья!
   Парень девушку домой
   Провожал с гулянья.
       Шли они — рука в руке,
       Шли они до дому;
       А пришли они к реке,
       К берегу крутому.

4. Позабыл знакомый путь
   Ухажор-забава;
   Надо б влево повернуть,
   Повернул направо.
       Льётся речка в дальний край.
       Погляди, послушай,
       Что ж ты, Коля, Николай,
       Делаешь с Катюшей!

5. Возвращаться позже всех
   Кате неприятно,
   Только ноги, как на грех,
   Не идут обратно.
       Не хотят они домой
       Ноги молодые . . .
       Ой, гармонь моя, гармонь,
       Планки золотые!

2. *Khata vstala vperedi,*
   Tëmnoe okoshko.
   Okh ty, stëzhka, pogodi,
   Protianis' nemnozhko!
       Ty potishe provozhai,
       Paren' seroglazyi,
       Potomu chto ochen' zhal'
       Rasstavat'sia srazu.

3. *Daite zh v ruki mne garmon',*
   Chtob sygrat' stradan'ia!
   Paren' devushku domoi
   Provozhal s gulian'ia.
       Shli oni—ruka v ruke,
       Shli oni do domu;
       A prishli oni k reke,
       K beregu krutomu.

4. *Pozabyl znakomyi put'*
   Ukhazhor-zabava;
   Nado b vlevo povernut',
   Povernul napravo.
       L'ëtsia rechka v dal'nii krai.
       Pogliadi, poslushai,
       Chto zh ty, Kolia, Nikolai,
       Delaesh' s Katiushei!

5. *Vozvrashchat'sia pozzhe vsekh*
   Kate nepriiatno,
   Tol'ko nogi, kak na grekh,
   Ne idut obratno.
       Ne khotiat oni domoi
       Nogi molodye . . .
       Oi, garmon' moia, garmon',
       Planki zolotye!

WHO KNOWS WHY

И КТО ЕГО ЗНАЕТ

words by M. ISAKOVSKY
music by V. ZAKHAROV

Ev-'ry   eve - ning near my
На за - ка - те хо - дит
Na za - ka - te_kho - dit

home___ A__ young lad   he comes strol - ling   by
па - рень Воз - ле   до - ма_ мо - е - го,
pa - ren' Voz - le   do - ma - mo - e - vo,

Not one   word__ does he say to__ me, He just   looks and winks his
По - мор - га - ет мне гла - за - ми И не   ска - жет ни - че -
Po - mor - ga - et mne gla - za - mi I ne   ska - zhet ni - che -

eye. Who knows why he's wink-ing,— What can he be
го. И кто е - го зна-ет,— За - чем он мор-
vo. I kto e - vo zna-et,— Za - chem on mor-

think-ing?— Oh, why is he wink-ing,— Oh, why is he wink-ing?—
га - ет, За - чем он мор - га-ет,— За - чем он мор - га-ет.—
ga - et,— Za - chem on mor - ga - et,— Za - chem on mor - ga - et.—

Fine
D.C. except last time

2. When I meet him at a party,
   Singing, dancing—he is gay.
   Later on when we say good night,
   He just sighs and turns away.
     Who knows why he's sighing.
     He's practically crying.
     Oh, why is he sighing,
     Oh, why is he sighing?

2. Как приду я на гулянье,
   Он танцует и поёт,
   А простимся у калитки,
   Отвернётся и вздохнёт.
     И кто его знает,
     Чего он вздыхает,
     Чего он вздыхает,
     Чего он вздыхает.

2. *Kak pridu ia na gulian'e,*
   On tantsuet i poёt,
   A prostimsia u kalitki,
   Otvernёtsia i vzdokhnёt.
     I kto evo znaet,
     Chevo on vzdykhaet,
     Chevo on vzdykhaet,
     Chevo on vzdykhaet.

3. When I ask him, "Why so gloomy,
   Doesn't life have joy for you?"
   "Oh, I've lost—" he murmurs sadly,
   "My poor heart—it's broke in two."
     Who knows why it's broken,
     He shows me no token.
     Oh, why is it broken,
     Oh, why is it broken?

3. Я спросила: «Что невесел?
   Иль не радует житьё?»
   «Потерял я — отвечает,
   Сердце бедное своё.»
     И кто его знает,
     Зачем он теряет,
     Зачем он теряет,
     Зачем он теряет.

3. *Ia sprosila: "Chto nevesel?*
   Il' ne raduet zhit'ё?"
   "Poterial ia—otvechaet,
   Serdtse bednoe svoё."
     I kto evo znaet,
     Zachem on teriaet,
     Zachem on teriaet,
     Zachem on teriaet.

4. Yesterday he sent by mail
   Two letters puzzling me so much.
   Every line just dots and dashes—
   I just think he's lost his touch.
       Who knows what he's saying,
       What game is he playing?
       Oh, what is he saying,
       Oh, what is he saying?

4. А вчера прислал по почте
   Два загадочных письма:
   В каждой строчке — только
       точки,
   Догадайся, мол, сама.
       И кто его знает,
       На что намекает,
       На что намекает,
       На что намекает.

4. *A vchera prislal po pochte*
   Dva zagadochnykh pis'ma:
   V kazhdoi strochke—tol'ko tochki,
   Dogadaisia, mol, sama.
       I kto evo znaet,
       Na chto namekaet,
       Na chto namekaet,
       Na chto namekaet.

5. I could never guess the riddle,
   I could never pass the test.
   Only for some reason my heart
   Is pining sweetly in my breast.
       Who knows why it's pining,
       What meaning divining?
       Oh, why is it pining,
       Oh, why is it pining?

5. Я разгадывать не стала,
   Не надейся и не жди.
   Только сердце почему-то
   Сладко таяло в груди.
       И кто его знает,
       Чего оно тает,
       Чего оно тает,
       Чего оно тает.

5. *Ia razgadyvat' ne stala,*
   Ne nadeisia i ne zhdi.
   Tol'ko serdtse pochemu-to
   Sladko taialo v grudi.
       I kto evo znaet,
       Chevo ono taet,
       Chevo ono taet,
       Chevo ono taet.

THROUGH THE VILLAGE

ВДОЛЬ ДЕРЕВНИ

words by M. ISAKOVSKY
music by V. ZAKHAROV

2. We never even thought or dreamed
   it could be done,
   That from every tree they'd come
   and hang a sun.
   That we all would get to know this
   happy feeling;
   That each one would have a star
   upon his ceiling.

2. Нам такое не встречалось и
   во сне,
   Чтобы солнце загоралось на
   сосне,
   Чтобы радость подружилась с
   мужиком,
   Чтоб у каждого звезда под
   потолком.

2. *Nam takoe ne vstrechalos' i vo sne,*
   Chtoby solntse zagoralos' na sosne,
   Chtoby radost' podruzhilas' s
   muzhikom,
   Chtob u kazhdovo svezda pod
   potolkom.

3. Rain is falling, wind is blowing
   But in the village we do not care,
   for we have light.
   Beauty, happiness and light flood
   our town,
   And the very heavens in envy look
   down.

4. (*Repeat first verse*)

3. Небо льётся, ветер бьётся всё
   больней,
   А в деревне — частоколы из
   огней;
   А в деревне — развесёлая
   краса,
   И завидуют деревне небеса.

4. (Повторить первый куплет)

3. *Nebo l'ётsia, veter b'ётsia vsё
      bol'nei,
   A v derevne—chastokoly iz ognei;
   A v derevne—razvesёlaia krasa,
   I zaviduiut derevne nebesa.*

4. (*Repeat first verse*)

CLOUDS HAVE RISEN
OVER THE CITY

ТУЧИ НАД ГОРОДОМ ВСТАЛИ

Moderately

Clouds o'er the cit - y have ris - en,_____
Ту - чи над го - ро - дом вста - ли,_____
Tu - chi nad go - ro - dom vsta - li,_____

Charged with a storm is the air._____ By the
В воз - ду - хе пах - нет гро - зой._____ За да -
V voz - du - khe pakh - net gro - zoi._____ Za da -

words and music
by P. ARMAND

bye s at your thresh-old,_____ And it may be_____ the last time._____
бой у по - ро - га,_____ И, быть мо - жет, _____ на- всег - да. _____
boi u po - ro - ga,_____ i, byt' mo - zhet,_____ na-vseg - da. _____

2. Darkening forces are whirling;
Full in the face flies the gale.
For country and home we are
    fighting,
Worker-soldier divisions—all hail!
  Chorus
  Long the way, dear, long the
  journey;
  Won't you come out, dearest
  mine?
  We will say our goodbyes at your
  threshold,
  Wish me well on the front line.

2. Чёрные силы мятутся,
Ветер нам дует в лицо.
За счастье народное бьются
Отряды рабочих бойцов.
  Chorus
  Далека ты, путь-дорога,
  Выйди, милая, встречай!
  Мы простимся с тобой у
  порога,
  Ты мне счастья пожелай.

2. *Chërnye sily miatutsia,*
Veter nam duet v litso.
Za schast'e narodnoe b'iutsia
Otriady rabochikh boitsov.
  Chorus
  Daleka ty, put'-doroga,
  Vyidi, milaia, vstrechai!
  My prostimsia s toboi u poroga,
  Ty mne schast'ia pozhelai.

3. Oh, how I want you, my darling,
My heart is quivering so.
I don't even know how it started;
But that I love you, I know.
  Chorus
  Won't you come to me, my
  darling?
  Stay and kiss me once more yet,
  And I swear to you no matter
  what, dear,
  That I never will forget.

3. Жаркою страстью пылаю,
Сердцу тревожно в груди.
Кто ты? Тебя я не знаю,
Но наша любовь впереди.
  Chorus
  Приходи же, друг мой милый!
  Поцелуй меня в уста,
  И клянусь, я тебя до могилы
  Не забуду никогда.

3. *Zharkoiu strast'iu pylaiu,*
Serdtsu trevozhno v grudi.
Kto ty? Tebia ia ne znaiu,
No nasha liubov' vperedi.
  Chorus
  Prikhodi zhe, drug moi milyi!
  Potselui menia v usta,
  I klianus', ia tebia do mogily
  Ne zabudu nikogda.

SONG OF GREETING

ПЕСНЯ О ВСТРЕЧНОМ

words by B. KORNILOV
music by D. SHOSTAKOVITCH

With movement

The morn - ing greets us with its
Нас ут - ро встре - ча - ет про -
Nas ut - ro vstre - cha - et pro -

cool - ness, ___ The riv - er greets us with a
хла - дой, ___ Нас вет - ром встре - ча - ет ре -
khla - doi, ___ Nas vet - rom vstre - cha - et re -

breeze. ___ And life o-pens up in its full - ness, And
ка. ___ Ку - дря - ва - я, что ж ты не ра - да Ве -
ka. ___ Ku - dria - va - ia, chto zh ty ne ra - da Ve -

sing - ing is heard o'er the trees. Don't sleep, a - rise, you
сё - ло - му пе - нью гуд - ка? Не спи, вста - вай, ку -
së - lo - mu pen' - iu gud - ka? Ne spi, vsta - vai, ku -

2. And joy sings a song for a greeting,
   A song without end in the air.
   And people laugh as they are
      meeting,
   The morning is sunny and fair.
      The sun shines brightly overhead,
      We'll make our hay.
      The land arises from its bed
      To greet the day.

3. The workers with labor shall greet
      us,
   As you to your friends cast a smile.
   The whole city comes out to meet
      us,
   It makes life seem doubly
      worthwhile.
      Beyond the city gates, 'tis said,
      In every way,
      The land arises from its bed
      To greet the day.

2. И радость поёт не скончая,
   И песня навстречу идёт,
   И люди смеются, встречая,
   И встречное солнце встаёт —
      Горячее и бравое,
      Бодрит меня.
      Страна встаёт со славою
      На встречу дня.

3. Бригада нас встретит работой,
   И ты улыбнёшься друзьям,
   С которыми труд и забота,
   И встречный, и жизнь —
      пополам.
      За Нарвскою заставою,
      В громах, в огнях,
      Страна встаёт со славою
      На встречу дня.

2. *I radost' poët ne skonchaia,*
   I pesnia navstrechu idët,
   I liudi smeiutsia, vstrechaia,
   I vstrechnoe solntse vstaët—
      Goriachee i bravoe,
      Bodrit menia.
      Strana vstaët so slavoiu
      Na vstrechu dnia.

3. *Brigada nas vstretit rabotoi,*
   I ty ulybnësh'sia druz'iam,
   S kotorymi trud i zabota,
   I vstrechnyi, i zhizn'—popolam.
      Za Narvskoiu zastavoiu,
      V gromakh, v ogniakh,
      Strana vstaët so slavoiu
      Na vstrechu dnia.

4. And with it to victory striving,
   You, our youth will advance.
   And new generations arriving
   Shall carry the torch with firm
      hands.
         Life rushes on—it streams ahead,
         Young heads turn gray.
         The land arises from its bed
         To greet the day.

5. With words pouring forth like a
      fountain,
   Announce to the world, "Truth is
      here."
   Go forward to conquer life's
      mountain,
   To meet toil and love year by year.
         This love of life, my curly-head,
         Will make life pay.
         The land arises from its bed
         To greet the day.

4. И с ней до победного края
   Ты, молодость наша, пройдёшь,
   Покуда не выйдет вторая
   Навстречу тебе молодёжь.
         И в жизнь вбежит оравою,
         Отцов сменя.
         Страна встаёт со славою
         На встречу дня.

5. Такою прекрасною речью
   О правде своей заяви,
   Мы жизни выходим навстречу,
   Навстречу труду и любви.
         Любить грешно ль, кудрявая,
         Когда, звеня,
         Страна встаёт со славою
         На встречу дня.

4. *I s nei do pobednovo kraia*
   Ty, molodost' nasha, proidësh',
   Pokuda ne vyidet vtoraia
   Navstrechu tebe molodëzh'.
         I v zhizn' vbezhit oravoiu,
         Ottsov smenia.
         Strana vstaët so slavoiu
         Na vstrechu dnia.

5. *Takoiu prekrasnoiu rech'iu*
   O pravde svoei zaiavi,
   My zhizni vykhodim navstrechu,
   Navstrechu trudu i liubvi.
         Liubit' greshno l', kudriavaia,
         Kogda, zvenia,
         Strana vstaët so slavoiu
         Na vstrechu dnia.

# Discography

(All reference numbers are to Monitor Records. A complete catalog of Russian recordings may be obtained by writing this firm at 10 Fiske Place, Mount Vernon, N.Y. 10550.)

PART ONE—FOLK SONGS

Along the Peterskaya Road	MF 300 or *MFS 762
Boundless Expanse of the Sea	MFS 302
• Cliff on the Volga	MFS 319 or MFS 520 or *MFS 762
Down the Volga River	MFS 337
• Dubinushka	MFS 520 or *MFS 762
Farewell to Happiness	MF 300 or *MFS 762 or MFS 770
• In the Meadow Stood a Little Birch Tree	*MFS 540 or MFS 566
In the Valley	MF 300 or *MFS 762
Kalinka (Little Snowball Bush)	MFS 422
• Little Bell	MFS 520 or MFS 474 or MFS 422
My Sweetheart	MF 351
No Sounds from the City are Heard	MF 351
Oh, You Dear Little Night	*MFS 597 or MFS 770
Slender Mountain Ash	MFS 302 or *MFS 597
Snow Flurries	*MFS 560
• Song of the Volga Boatmen	MF 300 or MFS 319 or MP 541
• Stenka Razin (From Beyond the Island)	MFS 520 or *MFS 762 or MFS 770
Village on the Road	MF 300
Why Do You Gaze at the Road?	MF 351

PART TWO—POPULAR SONGS

Clouds Have Risen Over the City	*MFS 590
Dark Is the Night	*MFS 597
Far Away, Far Away	*MFS 600
Katiusha	*MFS 590 or *MFS 597
Lonely Accordion	*MFS 590 or *MFS 597
• Meadowland	MFS 703
Moscow Nights	*MFS 590 or *MFS 597
My Heart	*MFS 597 or MFS 566
• Regimental Polka	*MFS 540
Should the Volga's Banks Be Flooded	*MFS 597
Silently	*MFS 597 or *MFS 371
Strolling Home	MFS 703
The Light	*MFS 597
Wait for Me	*MFS 597
• Wait for Your Soldier	MFS 520

Titles of Recordings (LPs) Referred to in Discography
(All records contain complete Russian texts)

MF	300	Ivan Skobtsov Sings Russian Folk Songs	*MFS	560	Songs of Old Russia
MFS	302	Russian Folk Songs	MFS	566	Marusia Sings Russian-Gypsy Songs, Vol. 2
MFS	319	Chorus of the Volga	*MFS	590	Moscow Nights: Russian Popular Hits, Vol. 1
MFS	337	A Festival of Great Russian Songs	*MFS	597	Yulya Sings Moscow Nights & Other Russian
MF	351	Russian Folk Songs			Hits
*MFS	371	Play, Balalaika, Play	*MFS	600	Journey into Russia with Yulya
MFS	422	Yulya Sings Kalinka & Other Russian Songs	MFS	703	Alexander Zelkin Sings Russian Songs
MFS	474	Kostya: Russian Gypsy	*MFS	762	Oh, Nastasya: Songs of Old Russia
MFS	520	Soviet Army Chorus & Band, Vol. 1	MFS	770	Old Russian Favorites: The Svetoslav
*MFS	540	Soviet Army Chorus & Band, Vol. 2			Obretenov Chorus
MFS	541	Soviet Army Chorus & Band, Vol. 3			

*These titles are also available on cassette.

• The song titles preceded by bullets (•) are among 19 selections available on a compact disc (MCD-61500) performed by the Soviet Army Chorus & Band.

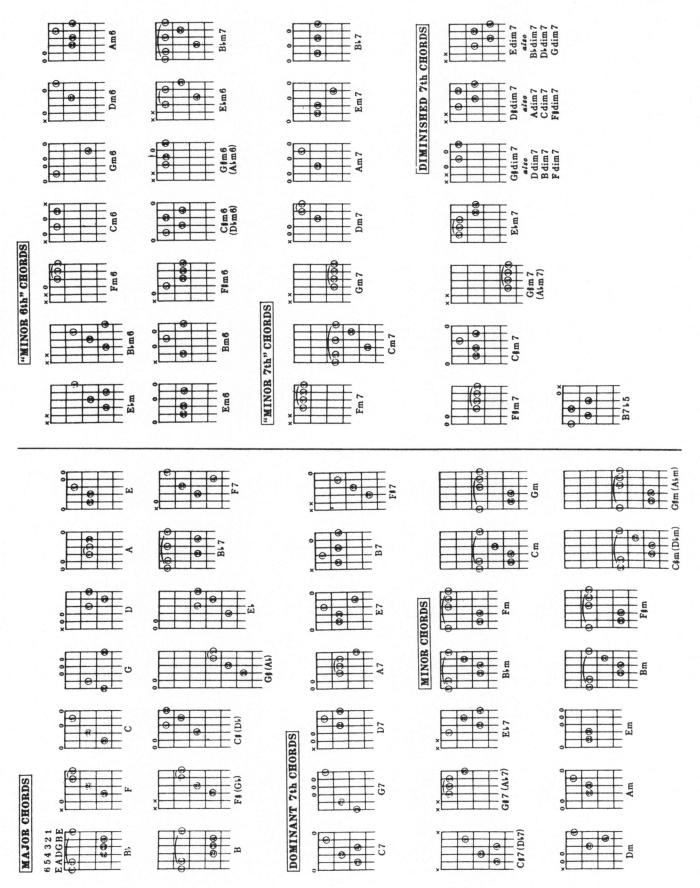